ARE YOU MISUSING OTHER PEOPLE'S WORDS?

Barbara Francis

COPYING

STEALING

CHEATING

PLAGIARISM

CUT AND PASTE

Enslow Publishers, Inc.
40 Industrial Road
Box 398
Berkeley Heights, NJ 07922
USA

http://www.enslow.com

For my husband and two daughters

Library of Congress Cataloging-in-Publication Data

Francis, Barbara, 1948-
[Other people's words]
Are you misusing other people's words? : what plagiarism is and how to avoid it / Barbara Francis.
pages cm. — (Got issues?)
Includes bibliographical references and index.
Summary: "Find out what plagiarism is, its history and how to avoid it"—Provided by publisher.
ISBN 978-0-7660-4321-3
1. Plagiarism—Juvenile literature. I. Title.
PN167.F73 2015
808.02'5—dc23
                    2013010584

Future editions:
Paperback ISBN: 978-1-4644-0587-7   Single-User PDF ISBN: 978-1-4646-1283-1
EPUB ISBN: 978-1-4645-1283-4   Multi-User PDF ISBN: 978-0-7660-5915-3

Printed in the United States of America
062014 Lake Book Manufacturing, Inc., Melrose Park, IL
10 9 8 7 6 5 4 3 2 1

To Our Readers: We have done our best to make sure that all Internet Addresses in this book were active and appropriate when we went to press. However, the author and publisher have no control over and assume no liability for the material available on those Internet sites or on other Web sites they may link to. Any comments or suggestions can be sent by e-mail to comments@enslow.com or to the address on the back cover.

♻ Enslow Publishers, Inc., is committed to printing our books on recycled paper. The paper in every book contains 10% to 30% post-consumer waste (PCW). The cover board on the outside of each book contains 100% PCW. Our goal is to do our part to help young people and the environment too!

Illustration Credits: AP Images, p. 62; AP Images/Jennifer Szymaszek, p. 30; Bettman/Corbis/AP Images, p. 67; ©Thinkstock.com, pp.: (Comstock, 5, 76; liquidlibrary, 79; Photos.com, 18, 20, 24); Official White House Photo by David Lienemann, p. 27; Shutterstock.com, pp.: (©arek_malang 43; ©auremar, 34; ©Diego Cervo 86; ©Gemenacom, 37; ©Helga Esteb, 65; ©Kamira, 3; ©leedsn, 51; ©Mariusz Szachowski, 45; ©Michaelpuche, 1, 71; ©Monkey Business Images, 53; ©Phase4Studios, 73, 89; ©Suzanne Tucker, 13; ©wavebreakmedia, 10, 84)

Cover Illustrations: Shutterstock.com /©Michaelpuche

Contents

What Plagiarism Is All About

Blair Hornstine had every reason to be optimistic about her future. It was the summer of 2003, and she had just graduated from high school in Moorestown, New Jersey. But she had done something just before graduation that had turned her into a very unpopular student, not only at her school but also throughout the whole town.

However, Blair would soon be leaving town and this controversy to start a brand-new life. She planned to start her freshman year at Harvard University, one of the most prestigious schools in the country, in the fall. Her brother had just graduated from Harvard and now she would follow in his footsteps.

Blair had earned excellent grades. She had done well on her SATs. She had worked with charities and won several scholarships. Despite what she had done in high school that made her so unpopular, Blair Hornstine had Harvard. No one could take that away from her.

And then someone did.

In early July, Blair received word that Harvard no longer wanted her. The university had taken the unusual step of revoking her admission—meaning they took it back.

One of the top colleges in the country had just told her she was no longer welcome. In addition, the story of her college rejection made headlines in newspapers and magazines all over the country.[1]

How could this happen?

It was not because, just before graduation, Blair gained notoriety by successfully suing her Moorestown, New Jersey, school district to be named the school's sole valedictorian rather than share the honor with another student. It was not because her lawsuit asked for close to $3 million in damages. It was not because her classmates and their parents had so turned against her over her lawsuit that she had refused to attend her graduation ceremonies. And, it was not because nearly twenty-seven hundred Harvard students signed an online petition asking the university to turn her away because of all of the above.

Harvard officials discovered something about Blair that summer that caused the university to change its mind about her. They were informed that Blair Hornstine had recently been caught plagiarizing several articles and essays she wrote for her local newspaper.

You may not know what plagiarizing is, but it is serious enough to have gotten Blair Hornstine kicked out of Harvard before she even got there.

This is how Blair committed plagiarism: She took words and phrases and passed them off as her own work in six of the seven articles she had written for her local New Jersey newspaper, the Cherry Hill *Courier-Post*.

Blair lifted words, sometimes whole paragraphs, from very lofty sources: a Thanksgiving proclamation issued by Bill Clinton when he was president, a written opinion by former Supreme Court Justice William Brennan, and an online article by a scholar from a Washington, D.C., foreign policy institute.

The *Courier-Post* printed a story that acknowledged Blair Hornstine's failure to attribute her source material. Attribution means to give credit to the people and places where you found your information. The newspaper also allowed Blair to write another article in which she said that she did not know that failing to credit other people's words and ideas is wrong.

Hornstine said this about her writing process: "When finalizing my thoughts, I, like most every teenager who has use of a computer, cut and pasted my ideas together. I erroneously thought that the way I had submitted the articles was appropriate. I now realize that I was mistaken."[2] She also claimed that she was unaware that the same rules that apply to citing sources for homework papers applied as well to writing newspaper articles.

Courier-Post Executive Editor Derek Osenenko says he was "certainly surprised" to learn that Blair Hornstine had plagiarized many of her stories. He said, "There was an understanding with everyone on the [writing] team to be original." He praised Blair for being "smart, analytical and focused" but admits that she "had a lapse in judgment."[3]

A major Philadelphia newspaper, *The Daily News*, jumped on the story and wondered how someone so smart could plead ignorance when caught plagiarizing. The newspaper also commented about Blair's lawsuit to be sole valedictorian, "Now it turns out that the girl who wouldn't share wasn't above stealing other people's words."[4]

Plagiarism Has Consequences

By all newspaper accounts of Blair Hornstine's dealings with Harvard, she was permitted to talk to university officials about her plagiarized material. Harvard's student handbook was very clear about plagiarism. It stated, "Students should always take great care to distinguish their own ideas and knowledge from information derived from sources." The handbook went on to say, "Students who, for whatever reason, submit work either not their own or without clear attribution to its sources will be subject to disciplinary action, and ordinarily required to withdraw from the College."[5]

Harvard has a policy of not discussing individual admissions problems and officials would not discuss Blair's situation with journalists. Though Blair Hornstine was not yet a Harvard student, university officials stood firm when reporters called them for comment.

The school has a very famous newspaper called *The Harvard Crimson*. A *Crimson* article quoted the school's director of admissions, who said that the university could revoke an admission if it questioned a prospective student's "honesty, maturity or moral character." The *Crimson* also quoted an unnamed source who said that it would be very unusual for Harvard not to act against an individual whose plagiarism was confirmed.[6]

Despite her explanations to the school, Blair Hornstine was turned away from Harvard.

How Does Plagiarism Affect Me?

The whole idea of plagiarism can be confusing, particularly as students begin to write more in-depth papers that require more complex research. Plagiarism should be openly discussed in a classroom so that the rules surrounding it become quite clear to all the students. As we saw in the case of Blair Hornstine, the consequences for not learning this can be very serious.

When someone plagiarizes, he or she is cheating. To plagiarize is to take work that is not your own and submit it as your own, without giving credit to the person who created it. Plagiarism is dishonest. Plagiarism is not only cheating, it is also a form of lying and a form of stealing.

Imagine spending weeks working hard on a homework paper only to have another student take the paper, put his name on it, and submit it as his own. You would feel that you had been cheated and the other student had stolen from you.

Plagiarizing can be even more confusing because the word can be applied not only to people who do it on purpose but also to those who do it accidentally. People plagiarize accidentally because they either do not know much about plagiarism or they just have sloppy work habits. For instance, if you forget to put quotation marks around a sentence you used from a library book, you are accidentally plagiarizing, but plagiarizing nonetheless.

Many students do not realize that presenting someone else's work as their own is wrong. But they do know about honesty. And they do know that stealing is wrong. The same way that you should not steal someone's wallet or CD or backpack, you should not steal another person's words and creative ideas.

Thomas Mallon has written a book about the history of plagiarism called *Stolen Words: The Classic Book on Plagiarism*. In his book, Mallon talks about how writers feel very possessive about their words: "Think how often, after all, a writer's books are called his or her children." He adds that writers whose works are plagiarized feel their words have been "kidnapped."[7]

Take a look at these paragraphs Blair Hornstine "kidnapped" and included in the articles she submitted to the *Courier-Post*, and then look at the original source material she borrowed from a former U.S. president.

For a Thanksgiving column she wrote:

> *As we celebrate Thanksgiving, let us remember with gratitude that, despite our differences, each of us is a member of a larger American family and that, working together, there is nothing we cannot accomplish.*[8]

9

The whole concept of plagiarism can be confusing to students. It's important to learn what's okay and what's not okay in using and citing sources.

Now take a look at a Thanksgiving proclamation issued in November 2000 by then-President Bill Clinton:

> *As we celebrate Thanksgiving, let us remember with gratitude that despite our differences in background, age, politics or race, each of us is a member of our larger American family and that, working together, there is nothing we cannot accomplish in this promising new century.*[9]

Blair Hornstine had options to choose from while writing her Thanksgiving article. She could have put quotation marks around those words and given Bill Clinton credit for having used them in his White House proclamation. Or she could have done more thinking and come up with her own words describing how she felt about celebrating the holiday. Either choice would have avoided plagiarism.

Do Your Own Thinking

When you lift the work of others and pretend it's yours, you are taking a shortcut through the learning process. That means you are not acquiring the critical thinking skills you should be learning. Those skills will help you later on in your education and in your adult life.

Think about this: Would you want to put your life in the hands of a doctor who cheated throughout medical school? Would you want to learn from a teacher who plagiarized all through college?

This book will give you an overview of what plagiarism is. It will show you how plagiarism appears in many forms. It can be as intentional as stealing entire paragraphs of someone else's work or as accidental as forgetting to put quotation marks around a sentence that you have not created yourself.

This book will help you sort out these ideas and show you how to avoid copying the work of others. It will show you how to properly conduct your research and how to move toward creating original work based more on your own, original thoughts.

Other Forms of Plagiarism

Though plagiarism is most often associated with the written word, it can also mean the theft of many other types of creative ideas: music, scripts, paintings, and designs.

When you go to the movies, notice that once the actual movie is over, you see rolling by on the screen a list of names next to the jobs those people performed while working on the movie. That list is called screen credits, and it is there to acknowledge the creative hard work those people contributed to the movie you just saw. Someone had to write the movie, someone had to direct it, and someone had to produce it. Someone even had to clean up the movie set.

Artists sign their paintings to receive credit for their work and to stake a claim to that particular piece of creativity. Notice that the cartoonist, who does not want other people stealing his ideas, signs the comic strips that you read in the newspapers.

Even something as sacred as a church sermon can be plagiarized. In late 2003, the Reverend Alvin O. Jackson, a well-known preacher from a large congregation in Washington, D.C., eventually resigned after he was caught plagiarizing his Sunday sermons.[10] One of his parishioners noticed that Jackson's speaking style had recently changed and that he was taking on new themes in his speeches. She typed the title of one sermon into a search engine and found the speech on a Web site belonging to the Reverend Thomas K. Tewell, a minister in New York City.

The Reverend Jackson finally admitted using sixteen of the Reverend Tewell's speeches without permission and without giving credit. In addition, the Reverend Jackson had bundled a bunch of these plagiarized sermons onto audiotapes and had the church sell them for fifty dollars each. The Reverend Tewell had taken the time to copyright his original speeches, which means he registered them with the U.S. Copyright Office in Washington, D.C.

Although someone who creates an original work, such as a speech, legally owns the work from "the moment it is created,"[11]

Research has found that a significant number of students admit to cheating on exams and written work, and the proportion has risen in recent years.

having copyright protection gives the creator proof of ownership should the creator want to sue someone for plagiarism. The Reverend Jackson got off lucky—he could have been sued by the Reverend Tewell. Jackson asked his parishioners for forgiveness and then took a leave of absence.

No matter what kind of creative idea is involved—written words, speeches, music, or design—the principle is the same. Presenting another person's work as your own is plagiarism.

Plagiarism Is on the Rise

The International Center for Academic Integrity (ICAI), housed at Clemson University in South Carolina, is one of several organizations that researches student cheating. ICAI was formed to work for honesty and integrity in the classroom. The organization is comprised of representatives from hundreds of schools and institutions from eighteen different countries. They work together, sharing information and ideas about how best to educate students to be honest in their schoolwork and to reject the temptation to cheat.

ICAI has discovered through its surveys that an alarming number of students are cheating. It has called the results of its studies "disturbing, provocative and challenging." The Center reported that in 2001, 41 percent of college students admitted to plagiarizing from the Internet—up from only 10 percent in 1999.[12] This was quite an increase. And the number continued to rise. Surveys done from 2006 to 2012 found that 60 percent of college students admitted to cheating in their schoolwork.[13]

ICAI's 2000 survey revealed that cheating was also a "significant problem" in high school. The study found that 72 percent of students admitted to "serious cheating on written assignments."[14] To understand this percentage, imagine three out of four of your friends cheating on a writing assignment. Or look at it this way: Only one in four students was turning in original work.

In the same 2000 survey of high school students, ICAI found that nearly half of the students questioned admitted they had "engaged in some level of plagiarism on written assignments using the Internet."[15]

Attorney Michael Josephson created another organization, the Josephson Institute of Ethics, to promote ethical behavior in young people. Every two years the institute conducts a nationwide survey of teenage students regarding their ethical behavior.

Its 2002 survey questioned thousands of high school and middle school students. The survey found that 74 percent of middle school students admitted to having cheated on a test.[16] Again, this means that more students had cheated than had not. Granted, cheating on tests is not plagiarism, but the figures show that more than half the students questioned admitted that, at least once, they were dishonest.

Rampant cheating in schools continued. In the Josephson Institute's 2010 survey, almost 60 percent of the students surveyed admitted to cheating on a test.[17] The institute also found that 34 percent of the students it interviewed admitted to having copied something from the internet for a school assignment.[18]

Just as revealing was the 81 percent of students questioned who admitted they had "copied another's homework," with 60 percent saying they had done so two or more times.[19] This behavior contradicts, though, what the students actually think of themselves: 98 percent of students on the survey said "it is important for them to be a person of good character." [20]

In addition, these same students seem to know what kind of ethical behavior is expected of them, especially from parents. The survey found that the vast majority of students, 92 percent, said that their parents or guardians "always want me to do the right thing, no matter the cost."[21] And only 8 percent said their parents "would rather they cheat than get bad grades."[22]

It is no secret that students sometimes feel that the emphasis rests on grades rather than learning, on the end result rather than

15

the process. And the busy schedules of today's students have them running from classes to soccer practice to piano lessons to karate classes and back home to the homework table. Stretched for time, a student with a term paper due the next day might think that borrowing someone else's words and ideas "just this once" might be OK.

Plagiarism and Technology

The two most beautiful words to a plagiarist's ears are these: search engines. The World Wide Web, which provides massive amounts of information at the click of a mouse, has produced a playground for plagiarists.

This method is tempting, especially for someone who is pressed for time. Not everyone has the skill—or the desire—to manage time. Slaving over a term paper that was assigned weeks ago but is due tomorrow is not an unusual occurrence. This age-old student dilemma has created a new industry in the last few decades: a number of Internet sites that provide fast, convenient, and customized term papers on just about any subject.

However, students should note one important fact when thinking about downloading other people's words off a Web site. If it is out there for students to find, it is out there for their teachers to find as well. Though teachers would rather teach than police, they are also capable of firing up their own search engines to catch students they suspect might be plagiarizing. All they have to do is type in a string of words from a student paper and their effort might reveal a grade-busting cut-and-paste job.

In this day and age, teachers have access to online services such as Turnitin.com that specialize in plagiarism detection. These services allow a teacher who suspects a student may have turned in unoriginal work to upload an entire paper and check it against an online data bank of millions of papers to see if the student has indeed plagiarized. The creators of these programs claim that they have taken the guesswork out of it for teachers. Some teachers feel that, for students, just the mere thought of being caught by their teacher's plagiarism detection program may curb plagiarism in the classroom.

While technology makes it easier than ever before to plagiarize, technology also makes it easier than ever before to get caught. But be aware that the message here is not: Do not cheat because you might get caught. The message here is: Do not cheat because it is the wrong thing to do.

Borrowing Through the Ages

Throughout history, people have borrowed ideas from other people. As far away in time as a couple of thousand years ago, in ancient Roman times, and as recently as three hundred years ago, the borrowing of plot lines and characters was not necessarily looked upon as a bad thing. Society once considered it the highest form of flattery to borrow. Writers, poets, and singing troubadours borrowed elements of stories, songs, and plays from other people, added new elements to them, and fashioned something new based on something old.

Most cultures valued following tradition more than creating original work. The public viewed writers as paying tribute when they borrowed ideas from writers who came before them—ideas that may have already been borrowed once before. This was prior to the mid-1400s, when the printing press was invented. This was also before laws were enacted providing copyright protection to authors. From ancient to medieval times, plagiarism as we see it today was not looked upon as a crime or as cheating.

The Romans told stories similar to those of the Greeks. Even in the Bible, words and ideas in the New Testament were borrowed from those in the Old Testament. For example, Matthew, Chapter 1, Verse 23, in the New Testament reads: "Behold, a virgin shall be with child, and shall bring forth a son, and they shall call his name Immanuel, which being interpreted is, God with us." Compare this with Isaiah, Chapter 7, Verse 14, of the Old Testament: "Therefore the Lord himself shall give you a sign; Behold, a virgin shall conceive, and bear a son, and shall call his name Immanuel."

Further down through history, Geoffrey Chaucer, one of England's most distinguished poets, borrowed heavily from Italian Renaissance writer Giovanni Boccaccio. Chaucer wrote his masterpiece *The Canterbury Tales* in the late 1300s, over six hundred years ago, while Boccaccio wrote *The Decameron* decades earlier. Both of these books include stories about the adventures of various people of the time whose experiences could be funny or show their human failings. And where did these writers get their ideas? Primarily from stories, known to us as "legends," told by people as they traveled on foot or horseback from village to village.

There was a time when borrowing plots and stories was an acceptable practice, especially if an author took a story line and turned it into something greater than the original. One of the most well-known examples of this surrounds the works of Greek philosopher Plutarch and English literary master William Shakespeare. Shakespeare is considered by many to be the greatest playwright of all time.

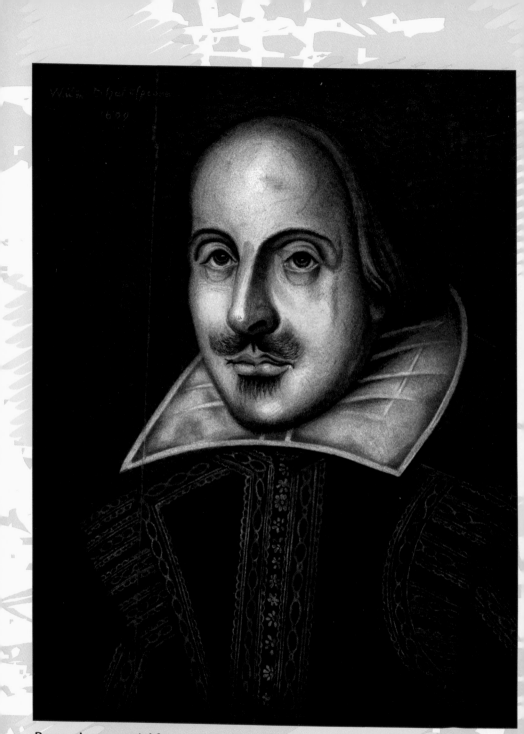

Borrowing material from other writers was an acceptable practice at one time. Nearly all of William Shakespeare's plots are taken from other writers.

Plutarch was born around 46 AD, about fifteen hundred years before Shakespeare's birth in 1564. Plutarch wrote a series of biographies under the title *The Parallel Lives*. Plutarch's biographies told the real-life stories of Greeks and Romans and how the character of these men affected their lives and their time. Plutarch's work influenced writers down through the ages.

Historians believe Shakespeare read Plutarch's stories after they were first translated into English in the late 1500s. Shakespeare used biographies from *The Parallel Lives* as source material for his plays about the ancient Romans, including *Julius Caesar, Antony and Cleopatra*, and *Coriolanus*.[1]

Plutarch's story of Julius Caesar is rich with details about the conquering Roman leader who was murdered in the Senate by a band of conspirators, and what happened to the murderers afterward. Shakespeare takes this story and brings it to life on the stage by plotting out five acts and giving these characters spellbinding dialogue as well as doubts, fears, and the countless weaknesses that make man what he is. Shakespeare did not copy Plutarch word for word. He took a true story from history, written about events that took place centuries earlier, as his jumping-off point and created something new and original—a literary masterpiece.

From Borrowed to Stolen

The word "plagiarism" comes from the Latin *plagium*, which means kidnapping. The *Oxford English Dictionary* lists the word "plagiary," derived from Roman times, to mean one who abducts (kidnaps) the child or slave of another. The word "plagiarism" also comes from the Latin *plagiarius*, or plunderer. To plunder means to seize or rob someone else's things by dishonesty or force.

One school of thought holds that with the invention of the printing press, borrowed ideas stopped being mere tribute to the original writer and became downright theft.[2]

Johannes Gutenberg, a German printer working in the mid-1400s, built the first printing press with movable type in Western

Europe. The Gutenberg Bible, printed on Johannes Gutenberg's press in 1455, is believed to have been the very first book printed from movable type in Europe. Prior to this, books were written by hand, which took a long time. Handwriting books, as opposed to mass-producing them on a printing press, meant that many fewer books were produced.

The invention of the printing press changed forever the way writers brought their stories to audiences. A printing press could produce many books quickly. The practice of slowly and laboriously writing books by hand disappeared. Because of the printing press, many more people could obtain copies of books and be exposed to the ideas in those books. The wider distribution of books helped to educate people in a world where many were illiterate.

Thomas Mallon writes about the invention of the printing press, "A modern world was printing and distributing itself into existence."[3] Around the late 1600s, writing became an actual profession, an actual trade, " . . . but in the new 'fellowship of authors' there was also a good deal of feuding and possessiveness. Things were now competitive and personal, and when writers thought they'd been plundered [stolen from] they fought back."[4]

With their words firmly printed on paper, writers began to believe they could actually own their words and ideas. The thought of being plagiarized, of someone stealing their "possessions," struck fear in the hearts of writers. Suddenly, it became important for writers to credit their sources and a bad thing not to do so. And society began to wonder if plagiarism was a crime, and if so, what should be done about it.

The First Copyright Law

United States copyright law has its roots in English copyright law. After the printing press was introduced in England in the late 1600s, more books were produced there. King Charles II decided to control the printing trade with the Licensing Act of 1662, which required that books had to be registered with a chosen group of printers called the Stationers' Company. These printers "were given powers to seize books suspected of containing matters hostile to the Church or Government."[5] While the last Licensing Law expired in 1681, the printing trade continued to be regulated.

After a change of monarchy in which Queen Anne now reigned, the British Parliament, the lawmaking arm of the government, created a law giving writers copyright protection of their books. In 1710, Parliament passed this law called the Statute of Anne. Under the Statute of Anne, an author would own a copyright of his book for a fixed period, fourteen years, to be renewed for another fourteen years if the author was still alive.[6] The law gave authors, instead of printers, the right to duplicate their work. Making and selling many copies of their books allowed authors to realize profits from these sales.

In the United States, after the Revolutionary War, when Britain no longer ruled the colonies, the new government modeled many of its laws after British laws. In 1787, the U.S. Constitution included a copyright provision in Article I, Section 8, Clause 8, that read, "the Congress shall have power . . . to promote the progress of science and useful arts, by securing for limited times to authors and inventors the exclusive right to their respective writings and discoveries."

In 1790, the First Congress implemented this copyright provision via a law with a very long name: The Copyright Act of 1790, an Act for the Encouragement of Learning, by Securing the Copies of Maps, Charts, and Books to the Authors and Proprietors of Such Copies.

Toward the end of the 1700s, attribution of sources (giving credit to where ideas came from) was fairly common. And that is when authors, some of them very famous, began accusing each other of plagiarism. Some of these accusations were probably true, while others may have been cases of professional jealousy.

In the early 1800s, famed English poet Samuel Taylor Coleridge, author of the poem "The Rime of the Ancient Mariner," accused poet Sir Walter Scott of borrowing from other authors for Scott's

Many great American writers were involved in plagiarism scandals. Edgar Allan Poe (shown here) claimed that Henry Wadsworth Longfellow had plagiarized. Others accused Poe of plagiarism as well.

poem "Lady of the Lake."[7] But Coleridge was not above borrowing himself. His biographer states that while many authors of the time freely borrowed from each other, "Coleridge was a special case. It is perfectly clear that between 1811 and 1816 he incorporated dozens of unacknowledged passages from German authors . . . in his lectures and published works."[8]

Later in the century, American writer Edgar Allan Poe launched a one-man crusade against plagiarism. Poe famously hurled plagiarism accusations against poet Henry Wadsworth Longfellow. His attacks on Longfellow in literary magazines were so relentless that a Poe biographer, Kenneth Silverman, referred to them as the "ongoing Longfellow War." Apparently Longfellow never defended himself publicly against Poe's many accusations. According to Silverman, "He considered life, he said, 'too precious to be wasted in street brawls.'"[9] At the same time, Poe was forced to defend himself against accusations that he plagiarized parts of his famous poem "The Raven."[10]

Most of these plagiarism accusations among literary giants never went anywhere beyond the accusation/denial stage and the attempt to make the other author, usually a competitor, look bad. But the stage was set by authors for ownership of words and ideas.

When Original Ideas Collide

Theories exist that there are only seven basic plots in literature. (Some say the number is twenty, others say it is thirty-seven.) The seven basic plots are: man (or woman) vs. man, man vs. nature, man vs. the environment, man vs. machines, man vs. the supernatural, man vs. self, and man vs. God.[11] An interesting phenomenon occurs on occasion when creative minds are at work. Two people can honestly and independently come up with the same idea at roughly the same time. People are capable of creating very similar works without either party being guilty of plagiarism. This is simply coincidence.

The Consequences of Plagiarism

Despite legal protection, there are few records in the early decades of copyright law of writers actually taking other writers to court over plagiarism. However, the record shows that in modern times, plagiarists have often suffered other, very serious consequences. Those who have been caught have been expelled from schools; fired or asked to resign from jobs, which resulted in lost income; pressed to give back prestigious awards; and instructed to pay money to people from whom they have plagiarized.

Some people's reputations have survived a plagiarism scandal, while others' have not. The following are a few modern-day examples of people caught plagiarizing and what they suffered as a result of their actions.

Plagiarism and Politics

In the summer of 1987, Senator Joseph Biden of Delaware wanted to become president of the United States. He was campaigning across the country, along with other Democratic candidates, to win the Democratic party's presidential nomination. Whoever won the nomination would run for president in the fall of 1988 against the Republican party's candidate.

In politics, competition is tough. Candidates need to seize the public's attention to communicate, in a passionate way, how they plan to lead the nation. Dull and boring candidates, even qualified ones, often have trouble getting people to listen to them.

Joe Biden was known for being a passionate public speaker. People listened to him and believed what he was saying. But his strong desire to be the Democratic party presidential nominee led him to commit a big mistake that eventually forced him out of the race.[12]

A *New York Times* journalist caught Senator Biden plagiarizing a speech during a campaign debate in Iowa. Biden had borrowed words and ideas from a speech, without giving credit, that was

Vice president Joseph Biden in his office. Plagiarizing the speech of a British politician nearly cost Biden the trust of the American public.

originally delivered with great passion earlier in the year by a politician in England named Neil Kinnock.

Look at samples below of both speeches. It is clear that Biden lifted Kinnock's ideas about descending from simple, uneducated people and being the first in his family to attend college. Biden also used some of the same wording that Kinnock used, changing words here and there to Americanize them for a U.S. audience. Borrowing words and ideas from someone else and presenting them as your own is plagiarism.

Here is a sample of candidate Neil Kinnock's speech:

> *Why am I the first Kinnock in a thousand generations to be able to get to university? . . . Was it because our predecessors were thick? . . . Was it because they were weak, those people who could work eight hours underground and then come up and play football, weak? It was because there was no platform upon which they could stand.*

Here is a sample of Senator Biden's speech from several months later:

> *Why is it that Joe Biden is the first in his family ever to go to a university? . . . Is it because our fathers and mothers were not bright? . . . Is it because they didn't work hard, my ancestors who worked in the coal mines in Northeast Pennsylvania and would come up after 12 hours and play football for four hours? . . . It's because they didn't have a platform upon which to stand.*[13]

It is common knowledge and generally accepted that politicians rarely write their own speeches, leaving this chore to professional speechwriters. In fact, an entire staff of White House speechwriters composes speeches for the president to deliver at public events. However, it is also generally accepted in the world of politics that politicians are responsible for what they say, no matter who wrote it. Senator Biden was no different.

To further embarrass Biden after *The New York Times* story exposed him, a rival politician's campaign released to reporters a video that actually showed parts of both speeches delivered by Kinnock and Biden. Once the question of plagiarism arose, Biden was found to have borrowed pieces of speeches from other politicians, including the late Senator Robert F. Kennedy. As a result, Biden took a bashing in the media and lost credibility (believability) in the eyes of the public. He was forced to withdraw from the presidential race. Joe Biden went on to serve many more terms in the U.S. Senate. But when he presented words as his own that were not his own, he lost the public's trust, and was no longer eligible in the eyes of Americans to become president. It would take many years for Biden to regain the public's trust enough to be thought of as a candidate for high office. He would be elected vice president in 2008.

Laurence I. Barrett, an author and former *TIME* magazine correspondent who covered the 1988 presidential campaign, looks back on the controversy:

"The moral of this story, and others like it is, that if you are in the public arena, a politician or a journalist or a speechmaker, you need to be scrupulous [very careful] in attributing what you say if someone said it first. There's a vulnerability to having your credibility challenged." Biden, Barrett says, made an error and "paid a pretty heavy price."[14]

Plagiarism and Journalism

The New York Times is one of the oldest newspapers in the United States. It began publishing in 1841. People all over the United States respect and value the news as printed in its pages.

In the spring of 2003, a twenty-seven-year-old *Times* reporter named Jayson Blair created what the *Times* itself described as the biggest internal crisis of its then 152-year history. Blair had been hired directly after college and was quickly promoted. In a few years, he became a national reporter. A national reporter covers stories all over the country that are of interest to people who live in every part

Jayson Blair, a reporter for *The New York Times*, plagiarized a number of stories by other reporters. He lost his job, as did two high-level editors at the *Times*.

of the United States. Blair was constantly filing stories for the paper, but he began to make a lot of mistakes in these stories. The *Times* was forced to print numerous corrections to many facts Blair had gotten wrong.

One day in April 2003, Robert Rivard, an editor of a Texas newspaper, the *San Antonio Express-News,* was reading an article in *The New York Times* written by Jayson Blair. It contained an interview with a grieving Texas mother whose soldier son had just been killed in the war in Iraq. This mother was describing how she felt and remembering the kindness of her son.

Rivard recognized her words. They had been printed in his newspaper days earlier as part of an article by one of his reporters. In fact, much of Blair's article had been lifted from the *San Antonio Express-News* article. Rivard complained to the *The New York Times.*[15] This complaint began the unraveling of perhaps the biggest string of journalistic plagiarisms in the history of newspapers.

At first, *The New York Times* defended Jayson Blair, believing his claims that he mixed up his notes. But then the paper's editors began looking at other Blair stories. They questioned him some more. They found he had not visited the cities he claimed to have been in and did not interview people he claimed to have met. Blair had never been to San Antonio. He had never met this grieving mother. He had taken advantage of an emotional story, a young soldier killed in war, to steal someone else's words to make himself look good.

Through the use of cell phones, laptop computers, and photos from the paper's library, Blair was able to give his editors the impression that he was on the scene covering a story when in fact he had not left New York. Then he would plagiarize another reporter's work to complete his articles.

Blair eventually confessed and resigned. The paper discovered Blair's fraud in thirty-six of the previous seventy-three articles he had written as a national reporter. Blair shattered the trust *Times* readers had in the paper. If his stories turned out to be false, a reader might ask, what else in the paper is also false?

The paper then printed a long article that gave the details of Blair's "frequent acts of journalistic fraud." The article said Blair's plagiarisms "represent a profound betrayal of trust and a low point in the 152-year history of the newspaper. . . . Mr. Blair repeatedly violated the cardinal tenet [most important principle] of journalism, which is simply truth."[16]

Though Jayson Blair later wrote a book about his days of deceiving *The New York Times*, the book did not sell very well. His few weeks of media coverage faded away. Blair has since faced his wrongdoing. He has worked to uncover the cause of his misconduct and help others who may find themselves in similar circumstances.[17] But no matter how hard he works to repair his reputation, he will probably always be remembered as having lied and cheated and hurt a lot of people.

As for *The New York Times*, its publishers had to do many things to put its house in order. They had to rid the newsroom of plagiarist Jayson Blair. They had to go back through all his articles and print corrections where Blair not only plagiarized but also made up facts and quotes. They had to ask for the resignations of two top editors, men with long and distinguished careers in journalism, who had been high-level bosses at the *Times* during Jayson Blair's days there. And they had to work for a long time to win back the trust and confidence of millions of *Times* readers.

In spite of these cautionary tales to journalists, writers continue to shortcut their research by cheating. One, Jonah Lehrer, is the author of three best-selling books. However, his 2012 book called *Imagine: How Creativity Works*, contained quotes that Lehrer had made up, but Lehrer had said were made by singer Bob Dylan, an American musician, singer-songwriter, artist, and writer.

Once these false claims were discovered, researchers began looking closely at other things Lehrer had written. The researchers soon found that Lehrer had self-plagiarised, or had re-used previous work he had written without saying that it had been published before.[18]

These incidents of cheating forced Lehrer to quit his job as a reporter for the well-known magazine *The New Yorker*. His book was pulled from bookstore shelves and people who had already purchased it were given a refund.[19] Lehrer may never be hired as a writer again.

3

The Temptation to Plagiarize

As students progress from grade to grade in school, they are constantly discovering the ideas of others. Most of these ideas will be new to them. That is what research and learning are all about. Part of the job for students is to process these new ideas through their own minds. They mix these new ideas with their own perceptions. A perception is how someone senses things.

The question for students to ask themselves is: How do I interpret the ideas of others and communicate what I have come up with in a creative way that I can call my own? Sometimes this is not easy. And the temptation to plagiarize becomes—for some people and for a variety of reasons—too hard to resist.

Plagiarism is the act of passing off someone else's work as your own. Students can commit plagiarism in two different ways: on purpose or by accident. Those who plagiarize by purposely stealing someone else's ideas are guilty of academic dishonesty. Those who plagiarize by accident should not feel shy afterward about asking the teacher for extra help. After all, to become skillful at citing sources when writing a paper is something that takes practice.

Students are learning about plagiarism at a much younger age these days. Many elementary school teachers teach lessons on what it is and how to avoid it. Students know that plagiarizing is wrong. It is taking the easy way out. It does not result in very much actual learning. In addition, a student who continually turns in "brilliant" work because he or she has copied from high-quality sources raises the achievement bar for others who are working very hard on their own, original work.

Students Understand Other Students

The following comments by middle and high school kids offer opinions as to why any student would want to plagiarize homework.

Ali, a sixth grader from Troy, Michigan, says: "[It's] because they want really good grades or they want people to like them." She adds, "[Maybe] it's because they don't like school. They may want to learn but they might not want to do the work."[1]

Her brother, Patrick, is a sophomore in high school. He says: "High school kids are lazy. They don't feel like getting up for school. Some people think they're not going to need half the stuff they learn in high school. [But] math and reading help you out getting a job."[2]

Lilli is a high school freshman in Los Angeles, California. She says: "Probably [it's] because they don't actually want to do the work. They're too lazy to do the work themselves."[3]

Matthew is a seventh grader from Fredericksburg, Virginia. He notes: "Maybe [it's] because they feel they can't write anything on their own and when they see this stuff, they think 'this is really good.'

They think what's written in a book is a lot better than what they'd do on their own."[4]

Author and teacher Robert Harris has similar views on why students plagiarize. In his book *The Plagiarism Handbook,* Harris says that some students just do not feel the need to work for their grades: "Many students are simply not convinced that the hard work required for a real education is worth it. . . . Some students believe that the diploma will be a magic ticket to a high-paying job regardless of what they learn, so that all the shortcuts they can find are appropriate."[5]

Excuses, Excuses

There are lots of reasons—or excuses—why students plagiarize. Teachers, parents, and school principals have heard most of them. The following is a list of excuses students sometimes use to explain why they have handed in other people's work as their own. Are some of these excuses familiar?

1. *I was in a hurry.* Time flies quickly for today's over-scheduled students, and sometimes they do not allow enough time to finish an assignment. Setting aside time to properly finish homework is called time management. It means thinking ahead to keep enough time available to complete a project. Time management takes some practice to master.

Suppose the teacher gives an assignment on Monday and says it is due in two weeks. That gives the students fourteen days to complete it. That is 336 hours. Somewhere in that 336 hours, after eating, sleeping, possibly working, playing sports, getting to and from school, taking music lessons, etc., there should be some time to put in on the assignment here and there. But it requires a little planning.

A student who sits down at her computer late Sunday night, after her parents think she has gone to bed, and starts work that is due the next morning, has not managed her time very well or given enough priority to her schoolwork. That is when it may become tempting

Among the excuses students give for plagiarizing are poor time management and the pressure to achieve.

to download a paper from the Internet or copy words right out of a book.

Ali says, "You should have done it earlier." She recommends that anybody who does not leave enough time to finish schoolwork "should ask the teacher for help"[6] instead of thinking about stealing someone else's work. In fact, teachers are probably more than willing to help out a student with time management. In addition, it is better to turn in an assignment late and possibly get a lower grade than to do something wrong such as plagiarize and then get a failing grade.

2. *I didn't know I wasn't supposed to.* Some subjects in school are easier than others. Some people prefer math, some prefer science, and others like geography. Some kids like to write. However, some kids—even some adults—find learning how to write essays and term papers to be difficult, and have trouble expressing their own creative ideas on paper.

The writing process actually begins with the research process— tracking down the source material that will be the basis for the new ideas highlighted in the paper.

There may be teachers who do not take enough time to walk their students through the process of researching and writing their papers. This process includes giving credit to others when their ideas and/or words are used. Some teachers may assume that their students know more about plagiarism than they actually do.

Even if someone does not know a lot about plagiarism, a simple rule to work by would be: If these are not my words, then I need to state where they came from. If in doubt, asking the teacher for guidance is always a smart thing to do.

Lilli thinks that high school students especially cannot claim that they did not know plagiarizing is wrong. "It's not really a good excuse if you get caught for this because you know you're not supposed to do this."[7]

Blair Hornstine tried to plead ignorance over lifting whole paragraphs from others. But Harvard officials most likely felt that a straight-A student about to graduate from high school at the top of her class must have known better. And for this, she lost her invitation to join the university's freshman class.

3. *There's pressure to get good grades.* It seems like there is always pressure from somewhere to get good grades. Some of this pressure comes from parents. Sometimes they do not realize how much stress they can cause by assigning too much attention to grades and not enough attention to what their kids are actually learning.

In addition, students can put pressure on themselves to compete for grades, attention, scholarships, and admission to good colleges. There is also a lot of competition among students to achieve. But the desire to achieve should not drive anyone to be dishonest.

Ali says this about handling pressure from parents, "I would say if you gave it your best shot, then your parents would still love you and you wouldn't need to copy somebody else's work."[8]

Matthew thinks that plagiarizing is "the same thing as looking over at somebody else's test paper. The point of a grade is an evaluation of how well you're doing."[9]

4. *Everybody else does it.* Parents often have an answer when a child wants to do something because everybody else does it. A parent might say, "If everybody went and jumped in the lake, would you do that too?" While there might be a lot of pressure from friends to do things just like they do and look just like they do, it is important to resist the temptation to cheat—if that is what they are doing.

Patrick has an opinion on this excuse to plagiarize. "I don't think everybody's doing it. That's just an excuse . . . because they know it's wrong and they shouldn't do it."[10]

Matthew says he does not know anybody who has plagiarized. "Most people I know can write stuff on their own without having to copy."[11]

Not everyone thinks that everybody else is plagiarizing. The 2010 survey by the Josephson Institute of Ethics, discussed in Chapter 1 of this book, found that "only 15 percent agreed that 'It's not cheating if everyone is doing it.'"[12] A vast majority of those students understood that "everybody's doing it" is not a valid reason.

But suppose a student has a close friend who is copying homework and enjoys "getting away with it" behind the teacher's back. That does not give anyone else the right to do it. Sometimes it takes just plain old hard work to get the assignment done.

5. *I mixed up my notes by accident.* Computers have now given us the ability to cut and paste other people's words into our notes and papers. Pulling something off the Internet and pasting it into one's own document without clearly identifying where it came from can lead to plagiarism.

Also, students who are sloppy about taking notes, who do not take the time to properly organize their notes and quotations, can commit plagiarism—before they even realize what has happened. This has even happened to professional writers who do not take time to separate and identify their sources as they are writing. A well-known author and historian who will be discussed in another chapter claimed, after she was accused of plagiarizing, that she had gotten her notes mixed up. (However, in her case, many reporters questioned how truthful this was once they learned how much she had borrowed.)

Lilli does not accept the excuse of mixing up notes. "I don't think they can get away with those excuses." She goes on to describe what is required at her school when using quotations. "Before you quote someone, you have to have an introducing sentence, then a colon."[13]

In terms of keeping notes organized, it is best for everyone to find a system that works for him or her, whether it is putting information onto colored note cards, using separate notebooks, or writing footnotes on each page as the term paper takes shape.

In a later chapter of this book, there will be information on how to properly organize research so that quotes, ideas, and whole paragraphs are not accidentally submitted to the teacher as original work.

6. *Somebody else said it so much better.* When teachers give out writing assignments, they have several goals in mind. They want to make sure students understand the material they are studying.

They want students to let them know what they learned—in their own words. They want students to form their own ideas about the subject. And teachers want their students to learn proper methods for conducting research.

Simply copying other people's words does not get any of these jobs done. When people learn to write with their "own voice," they are learning to think. The teacher ultimately wants to know what her student knows about the subject.

Ali comments about what teachers want: "They're not looking for what somebody else said better than you. The teachers are looking for what you think—and your parents are too."[14]

It is important to notice when downloading information from the Internet or copying material out of a library book, that someone else's writing style is different from your own. And, it may often be better. In cases when a scholar, an expert who has studied a certain subject for years, has written the material, that person will more often than not have a more polished writing style and use bigger words than what students usually turn in.

When finishing a paper, notice the quality of the writing. If some of it is much more complicated than what you are used to turning in, then those words and ideas probably did not originate in your own head. And the teacher can tell. Remember this: Someone may have said it better, but the teacher wants to hear from you.

7. *I'm not hurting anyone.* In fact, plagiarism can hurt a lot of people. Someone who plagiarizes part of a book is stealing from the original author. An author may have spent years researching and writing the book. Authors want credit for their hard work and original ideas, and they also want to sell their books.

Patrick says the idea that no one is getting hurt is not a very good excuse. "Because they know it was wrong. A person who did the work would feel bad because the person copied it and put their name on it."[15]

Handing in a purposely plagiarized paper is a form of lying to the teacher. It is wrong and damages the trust a teacher has in a student.

Most parents would also be upset to learn that their son or daughter had cheated.

When students plagiarize, they are missing out on a learning experience. Patrick says the person the plagiarist is hurting the most is "yourself. Because you didn't learn anything and you'll get punished for it."[16]

Matthew agrees that students turning in someone else's work hurt themselves the most. "Because you're not getting an education or anything from it, which is the point of it. You're not doing anything when you plagiarize. You're not helping yourself learn or understand. You're just doing nothing."[17]

Patrick has advice on the best way to learn. "Do your own work."[18]

8. *We do it in my country.* In some countries, students may be taught that copying another writer is a sign of respect for that writer. Furthermore, some cultures see the writing produced by its people as belonging to everyone. Plagiarism, therefore, is an unfamiliar idea.

In addition, the rules for citing sources in other countries may be very different than the rules in U.S. schools. These differences can lead to plagiarism troubles for students from other countries, especially if they are struggling to learn English.

For many students from other countries, avoiding plagiarism is a matter of learning what it is. They need to be taught the rules of citing sources that are expected of them in a new culture.[19]

Ali says, "You need to learn what we do in our country and not copy someone's work. In our country we consider it bad. Here it's not a compliment."[20]

Lilli adds, "I'd say to them that you don't want to get off on the wrong foot. I'd suggest if they don't understand . . . they can get help from teachers or some other students to tell them exactly what they're supposed to do so they can actually comprehend the work."[21]

Students who studied somewhere where the rules are different should work to understand what is required of them in an American

Most students understand that doing their own work is an important part of learning.

classroom. The possibility that students from another country may plagiarize by accident makes it even more important for teachers to create lessons on what plagiarism is and how to avoid it. And it is just as important for kids who were born in the United States to support their foreign-born classmates as they learn the rules in their new country.

Think Twice Before Plagiarizing

Most of the excuses listed above offer no concrete reason for anyone to plagiarize. All four students who commented on these excuses thought they were just that—excuses in place of not doing the work properly. Copying is not learning, nor is it understanding. Nor does it give students the satisfaction of creating something unique, something to call their own.

A university library director who has dealt with campus plagiarism issues believes this: "Students need to understand the significance of ownership in terms of their own written material." She adds that once this happens, "they come to understand the meaning of respect for intellectual property because they themselves have participated in its creation."[22]

Michael Josephson likes to remind students why it is important to turn in original work. "When you're in school, you're supposed to be developing certain skills. So the purpose of evaluation in schools is judging your competence. It's supposed to reflect your ideas." As for the temptation to plagiarize, Josephson adds, "You know what you're supposed to do with temptations. You overcome them."[23]

Plagiarism and the Internet

4

Today, with the click of a mouse, the Internet brings the world's knowledge right to your computer screen—knowledge that is all conveniently researched and presented by someone else. However, with all this information floating out there in cyberspace, some people believe they can take it and use it as they please.

Robert Boynton, who teaches journalism at New York University, has described this thinking as the "Napsterization of knowledge." Napster was one of the first computer programs that enabled people to download music for free and then share it with others. In most cases, downloading copyrighted music without paying for it is illegal. It is stealing. But, Boynton says, the constant practice of doing it may have blurred the line, especially in the eyes of young people, of what is right and what is wrong.[1] It may have led some people to think, "If it is there and it is free, then it is mine."

Here is why, briefly stated, downloading music for free from the Internet is wrong. Music is an artistic work created by someone. Most songwriters copyright their music and charge money to people who want to produce it as a song. The artist who owns the music, the singer who records the song, and the record company that packages and distributes it all expect to be paid for their work. That is how these professionals make their living. That is how a record company stays in business. They all receive a percentage of the small fee paid by music lovers who download music from the Internet. But freely taking artistic material, such as songs from a CD that are really for sale, is stealing.

Sharing illegally downloaded music seems to have decreased in the last decade. Some researchers feel that this is because music files have become less and less expensive and the number of music streaming sites such as YouTube and Spotify have increased. These methods of listening to music appear to have attracted more listeners because they are easy and convenient.[2]

Although illegal music downloading is falling, a growing number of students seem to feel it's ok to download knowledge from the Internet. Free information can sometimes beckon an overworked student. And this plentiful, convenient research available to students who want good grades but not willing to put in the hard work, has created a generation of bold plagiarists.

Back in the old days—back in the early 1990s, let's say— students who wanted to cheat by plagiarizing had to do it the old-fashioned way. They had to trudge to the library and copy phrases from source books or borrow a paper already written by a friend or an older sibling. For years, many college fraternity and sorority houses around the country have kept file cabinets full of term papers that their members could turn in as their own work.

But the rise of the Internet has created a whole new opportunity for plagiarists. In the words of Jayson Blair, "…the Internet was not as powerful a resource—or temptation—as it is today. It's so much easier to plagiarize under pressure today…"[3]

All a student has to do is log on to any search engine or essay site, type in a phrase or a few key words, and presto! In a matter of seconds, that student will discover a whole batch of Web sites practically begging him or her to sample its product.

Cybercheating Is Still Cheating

Take a few moments to brush up on your knowledge of medieval history by reading the following passage:

> *In 1494 the armies of the French king, Charles VIII, invaded Italy to capture the kingdom of Naples. They swept through the country and bombarded and destroyed many castles. This invasion signaled the end of the castle as a stronghold of defense. For centuries it had been the dominant fortification in Western Europe for the defense of kings, nobility, and townspeople. . . .*
>
> *A typical castle was usually guarded on the outskirts by a surrounding heavy wooden fence of sharp-pointed stakes called a barbican. . . . During an attack, large stones were thrown or boiling oil poured from the balconies onto anyone trying to climb the wall.* [4]

This is an interesting essay about what medieval castles were like and how they were used. But perhaps the most interesting thing about this essay is that it was downloaded for free from a popular Internet site that provides papers at no charge on just about any subject imaginable.

Anyone with access to the Internet can download this paper and turn it in as one's own. The site does not indicate who wrote the paper. It just lists five books and their authors as source material. It could be a plagiarized paper. But it is there for the taking. And its very existence can tend to make students, in the privacy of their own homes or dorm rooms, allow ethics—and their nagging conscience—to fly out the window.

Ellen Laird, a community college English instructor in upstate New York, believes that "we all pay the price" when it comes to Internet plagiarism. In an article she wrote for *The Chronicle of Higher Education*, a magazine for educators, Ms. Laird relates how she caught her student plagiarizing from the Internet.[5]

Ms. Laird noticed that a student, whom she calls Chip, turned in an essay that she described as more mature and focused than she had seen in his previous papers. His paper also discussed experiences unlikely to have happened to an eighteen- year-old. She used the search engine Alta Vista and, in just sixty seconds, found Chip's essay on an Internet essay site.

She was disappointed in Chip because she had discussed plagiarism and its consequences with her class on several occasions. She confronted him. He offered only lame excuses—he had waited until the last minute, wrote something he did not like, and then turned to the Internet for something better.

"But I sensed that Chip felt that he had made a choice akin to having a pizza delivered," she writes:

"He had procrastinated on an assignment due the next day, had no time left in which to prepare his work from scratch, and had to get on to those pressing matters that shape the world of an 18-year-old. He dialed the Internet service provider, ordered takeout and had it delivered."[6]

Do Not "Download Your Workload"

The digital age in which we now live has indeed created a large market for "academic takeout." Dozens of Web sites offer research papers for hundreds of topics. Some of them offer papers for free, some of them offer a free paper in exchange for another paper, and some of them charge a fee. Some of the sites provide space for users to rate the qualtiy of their papers.

The cost of these papers varies from about five to fifteen dollars a page. Most of these Internet "paper mills," as they have come to be called, will take all major credit cards. (Even, undoubtedly, cards that belong to unsuspecting moms and dads.) Some offer outlines, bibliographies, and different prices for different quality papers.

The paper mills will also fax, e-mail, or snail-mail a paper on request on just about any topic. They will, for a larger fee, overnight ship their papers. One paper writing company even advertises that its service offers newly written papers to keep students from getting into "serious trouble for turning in a plagiarized paper."[7]

Internet Sites Encourage Plagiarism

The following is a description of some well-known Internet sites that make up the busy online homework industry.

One site tells students that writing is a skill developed "over time through practice." It goes on to say that often students do not have time to do the research and careful writing needed for good papers. It then tells students that while they cannot buy time, they can buy an essay. It even encourages this kind of cheating by saying, "This is the most practical course of action when you're buried in a mountain of writing assignments and don't have the inclination to write one."[8]

This Web site will take custom orders for writing essays, research papers, admission essays, and even scholarship essays.[9] Imagine winning a scholarship based on someone else's writing! This adds a dimension of stealing money, not just ideas, to plagiarism.

Another popular paper mill site has been up and running since 1994 and brags on its home page about its library of over forty-five thousand essays.[10] You can search for a topic by clicking on to general links such as economics or criminal justice or oceanography.

Or, you can go right to a specific topic by typing in a few key words such as "Boston Tea Party," at which point the offer of several different papers immediately pops up. A link to their price pops up with them: the price for a ten-page essay is $9.95 per page, or $99.95. Furthermore, it promises same day delivery.[11]

This site will also provide what it calls custom work. This means a student who cannot find a perfect fit out of forty-five thousand choices offered on the site can special order a term paper on a very specific topic. The student just completes a form and someone somewhere will conduct the research and write the paper. It may be fast and easy—but it is wrong.

Another busy Internet site, the one with the advertising line, "Download your workload," brags that it offers one hundred thousand essays. This site, like most others of its kind, includes statements that tell students that the papers are not to be turned in as the student's own. This site states that "Plagiarism is NOT cool." It says that its papers are only "to help you learn, to clear things up you really don't understand, and to find resources where you can locate additional info."[12] These statements, however, seem to be nothing more than disclaimers—statements that keep the Web site from getting into trouble when a student uses its product to cheat.

Finally, there are Internet sites offering students information to help them better understand literary works such as books, poems, and plays. Some sites, including Sparknotes.com and Cliffsnotes.com, specialize in explaining these works. For instance, typing in a search for the book *To Kill a Mockingbird* at one of these sites provides the user with a chapter-by-chapter summary of the plot, a description and analysis of the characters, a short biography of the author, and a discussion of the book's themes. Teachers may not always like the fact that their students are consulting these sites, but the sites do provide additional help when a student is trying to understand what a novel is all about. A smart student will absorb the information rather than plagiarize.

However, there are other so-called book note sites that students should avoid because, in addition to offering information on literary

Because downloading material from the Internet is so quick and easy, students sometimes forget that it is unethical.

works, they also provide multiple links to paper mill sites—and a temptation to plagiarize.

Online Cheating Has Consequences

Michael Josephson of the Josephson Institute of Ethics acknowledges that "plagiarism has become so much easier technologically. It feels so risk-free." He says, "I don't think they [the students] feel the same sense of dishonor that they would if they were cheating on an examination." But Josephson adds that "plagiarism has become so much easier to detect."[13] And detection has consequences for the plagiarist.

College teacher David McGrath relates his experiences with detection and punishment. He was teaching an Internet-based composition class when a student e-mailed him to request a change of research topic to the Cherokee Indian relocation experience. McGrath allowed the change, but he knew there were essays all over the Web about this topic and suspected that his student was about to turn in a downloaded paper.

He describes what he went through to confirm his suspicions:

> I had to become a detective, spending hours copying excerpts from her paper into cheater catching software programs and search engines to verify that it was authentic. When I had proof that it was not, which happens about 30 to 40 percent of the time, I failed the student in a mixture of anger and pleasure . . . pleasure for nabbing a criminal and anger for her having wasted both our time.

McGrath says he found it much easier to fail a student he only dealt with electronically. "She pled ignorance, begged for another chance, swore she learned her lesson, even apologized. But I didn't care."[14]

This is a harsh example of the consequences of plagiarism, but it shows that some teachers take a very hard line with students who pull their papers from the Internet.

Plagiarism's Cousin: Fabrication

In the spring of 2004, twelve-year-old Ryan Templeton was studying Egypt under the pharaohs in his social studies class at North Belvedere Middle School in Brunswick, Illinois. Ryan did not care much for social studies. He was more interested in playing basketball and computer games. He found the ancient Egyptians boring.

Ryan liked his teacher, Mrs. Longo. She was nice and tried really hard, but he just could not get behind the history thing. He could not understand how dead people who lived thousands of years ago made any difference to his life.

Mrs. Longo assigned the class to write short papers on the Egyptians. Ryan had no interest in the assignment, but he wanted to please Mrs. Longo because he liked her. He decided he wanted to write about mummies, those dead bodies the Egyptians used to preserve and wrap in cloth, then bury inside the pyramids. Ryan had once dressed up as a mummy for Halloween. He thought if he had to turn in a paper on something, writing about mummies would be cool. Mrs. Longo sensed Ryan's excitement over mummies and agreed to let him write about them.

The next day, Ryan asked Mrs. Longo if he could change his topic to how the Great Pyramid was built. Mrs. Longo was puzzled but pleased that he was still interested in the subject. She said OK and looked forward to seeing what Ryan, who did not like to write papers, would turn in.

What Mrs. Longo did not know was the real reason Ryan had asked to change his topic from mummies to pyramids. Ryan had secretly found an old paper at home that had been written by his brother, Tom, who was several years older. Tom's paper was on the Great Pyramid, and he had gotten an A on it. Tom had just gone away to college and would not even know.

Ryan retyped the paper into a document file on his computer. He changed a word here and there. He spiced up the paragraphs by cutting and pasting information about Egypt that he downloaded from the Internet.

Ryan was pleased with himself when he turned in his paper. He told Mrs. Longo how he had enjoyed studying history for the first time.

After school, Ryan bragged to his best friend about what he had done and told him that the kids who spent hours writing their own papers were nothing but "suckers."

Several days later, Mrs. Longo asked Ryan after class if there was anything he wanted to tell her about his paper. He said no. She told him his writing this time was different from other writing he had turned in. He told her he had just worked on it extra hard. Then she informed him that she recognized his paper because she had been his brother's teacher several years earlier and she remembered it as mostly Tom's work.

Ryan was busted. The teacher gave him an F. He had to face not only the principal, but also his parents, who grounded him for a month.

The Plain Truth

Now that you know about Ryan Templeton, here are a few more things to know about him. He does not exist. His teacher does not exist, nor does his school or his town in Illinois. They are totally made up.

Do you feel deceived? You should, because you have been fed a made-up story.

A dictionary will tell you that to *fabricate* means "to make up in order to deceive." Inventing a story from scratch, including the characters, the setting, and the incidents, is called fabrication. Fabrication is a close cousin to plagiarism because it, too, is based on a lie and intentionally tries to deceive an audience.

Like plagiarism, fabrication is wrong. Fabrication differs from plagiarism in that it is often original work. It just is not true. Fabrication can take as much effort as researching and reporting something that is true. So why do people go to all the trouble of fabricating a story and risking the consequences? Maybe some students do not have enough confidence in their own research and reporting skills. Maybe they want to impress a teacher and turn in the best paper of the class. Or maybe, they secretly feel good about themselves only when they deceive others.

Teen Fabrication

The following is true; it is about a fabricated story that was discussed one morning on the television interview program *The View*.[1] One of the hosts of the show read a letter from a viewer who wrote that her daughter had recently been accepted to the college of her choice. However, this mother had just seen the essay her daughter had been required to write to submit with her college application packet.

The college asked applicants to write an essay about an event in their lives that had deep meaning for them. This woman's daughter had written a long and moving essay about the death of her brother and how she coped with this loss.

The trouble was, the mother wrote, her daughter had never lost a brother. She had never even *had* a brother. The daughter had completely made up the story for her essay, including all the terrible emotions she had gone through. The daughter had fabricated a story and presented it as fact. She had tried to dazzle the college application board with her writing—and maybe win a little sympathy with her sad story. She had cheated in order to get into the college of her choice.

The girl's mother had written the letter to *The View* because she was very distressed about what her daughter had done. She asked their opinion. One host thought it might be OK if the college was just testing an applicant's writing ability. But most of the other hosts thought that what the daughter had done was wrong.

Fabricating an essay is being dishonest. Do you think it is worth being dishonest in order to get into a good college? What do you think this girl's mother should have done when she discovered her daughter's deception? What do you think the college should have done if officials had caught the daughter pretending on paper that a sudden death in the family had changed her life forever?

A Look at Hoaxes

Like fabrication, a hoax involves a made-up story intended to deceive people. However, a hoax is more often than not intended to be funny and lighthearted and not to hurt anyone. It is designed to capture the attention of lots of people by presenting the fabricated story, often outrageous, in a serious manner.

A hoax plays to people's gullibility. A gullible person is easily deceived. The word "hoax" is thought to be derived from the word *hocus*, from the term *hocus pocus*, a phrase magicians use while performing their tricks.[2]

Quite often a hoax can be an April Fools' joke played on an unsuspecting public. National Public Radio (NPR) broadcasts an April Fools' Day story every year. For example, in 2004 NPR announced that the U.S. Post Office was planning to allow people to take their zip code with them when they moved.[3] The story noted that people become attached to their zip code. Some people use their zip codes as a symbol of wealth and prestige—think 90210 of Beverly Hills fame—so why not make zip codes portable? Of course, the story was completely false, but NPR had fun with it and hoped that its listeners did too.

There was a famous Halloween hoax in the United States in 1938 that sent some radio listeners into a panic. It started as about 6 million people listened to the usual evening fare of orchestra music on the CBS Radio Network. The broadcast was interrupted by announcements about a spaceship that had landed from Mars. Three-legged Martians had supposedly emerged from their ship and were using ray guns to kill anyone and anything in their paths— including seven thousand soldiers fighting to the death. The situation was dire.

Some people packed up provisions and drove from their homes. Others hid in cellars. Still others prepared to fight the invaders from outer space. What some people had not heard, especially those tuning in late, was an announcement at the broadcast's beginning that the Martian story was a dramatization by actor Orson Welles and his Mercury Theatre group of H. G. Wells's novel *War of the Worlds*.

This radio drama was, in fact, never intended even to be a hoax. But Orson Welles had made the program so realistic that people believed it.[4]

People may not let the radio scare them anymore. But we now live in the Internet era. An Internet hoax can sometimes take on a life of its own as millions of people have easy access to it and can pass it along to others in any form they wish. This process is a high-tech version of passing a constantly changing story along from ear to ear while sitting around the campfire.

Have you ever heard about the move to ban the substance dihydrogen monoxide? There has been an Internet movement to ban the substance because it has infiltrated every aspect of our lives. Among other things, dihydrogen monoxide as a contaminant is found in acid rain as well as in our lakes and streams. It can corrode things it touches. It is used in animal research.

The substance is all around us because the substance dihydrogen monoxide is . . . water.

In 1997, a fourteen-year-old Idaho junior high school student named Nathan Zohner used the premise of this Internet hoax for his science project. He gave a report on dihydrogen monoxide to fifty ninth graders and then took a survey. According to reports of his project, most of those surveyed favored banning the substance, a few were undecided, and only one student recognized the substance as water. By bringing to light the power of a science hoax, Nathan Zohner won first prize in his town's science fair that year.[5]

Fabrication and the Press

The examples above show how a made-up story as a hoax can be fun and mostly harmless. But a serious, fabricated story in the newspaper or on the TV news can be hurtful and ruin someone's reputation. Journalists can sometimes be tempted to fabricate stories because their editors expect them to produce many stories on very tight deadlines. Also, they are under pressure to tell stories that grab the public's attention. Most journalists honor the ethics of their trade and would not think of deceiving their readers. But on occasion, a journalist who cannot find a good story, or refuses to look for one, will simply invent one. Oddly enough, fabricating a good story can sometimes take as much time as searching for a genuine one.

Journalists who have been caught claim they have fabricated stories for many reasons. Some of them wanted to make their pieces more interesting and shocking, even if they were not true. Some of them made up great stories to win prizes and promotions and to earn pay raises.

Present-day journalism, both print and broadcast (radio and television), involves a lot of money, as well as millions of readers and viewers. There is strong competition to grab those readers and viewers. Sometimes journalists as fabricators cross a line of dishonesty that they cannot uncross.

Fabrication and Journalistic Integrity

Two episodes of journalists fabricating stories for well-known publications stand out in recent times. The following stories describe how these journalists betrayed the trust of their readers and their editors.

In 1998, Stephen Glass was an ambitious magazine writer who, by the age of twenty-five, had already published dozens of stories. He wrote for publications such as *The New Republic*, a well-known political magazine based in Washington, D.C., and *George*, a magazine no longer in business whose publisher was John F. Kennedy, Jr.

Stephen Glass went to great trouble to deceive his editors and the magazine's fact-checkers. Magazines and newspapers employ fact-checkers to look over a reporter's article to make sure all the names, dates, places, and stories are true and accurate. Glass forged fake notes, invented fake organizations he claimed he contacted, typed up fake news releases from those organizations, and made up fake people he said he interviewed.

Glass wrote a lot of stories very quickly. Sometimes his stories were hard to believe—so hard to believe that editors finally grew suspicious. One story told of a fifteen-year-old teenage hacker who broke into the computers of a big software company and then demanded, among other things, money and a sports car.[6] The incident never happened and the software company did not exist. After a reporter for *Forbes Digital Tool*, an online magazine, wrote that he could not find any proof of any of the claims Glass made in this story, Glass's editor, Charles Lane, finally confronted him. He made Glass drive him to the building where Glass had claimed a computer hackers' conference had taken place. Glass finally caved in and admitted his fabrications.

Glass's editors discovered that he had fabricated parts or all of twenty-seven of the forty-one articles he had written for *The New Republic*.[7]

After Glass confessed, other magazines he had written for took a closer look at his work and discovered more fabrications. One Glass story about powerful Washington lawyer Vernon Jordan, which ran in *George* magazine, contained so many lies that publisher John F. Kennedy, Jr., wrote a letter of apology to Jordan.[8]

Glass lost his job, his income, and his credibility. He suffered public humiliation when other journalists wrote terrible things about him. He went into hiding. He wrote a book about his deceptions, and a movie was released in 2003, *Shattered Glass*, that told his story. What was really shattered, though, was the complete trust his editors and readers placed in him.

Journalist Charles Lane, who was Glass's editor at *The New Republic* when the fabrications came to light, looks back on what those lies really cost Stephen Glass. "All of Stephen's friends felt personally betrayed, and have since turned their backs on him completely. So he forfeited an entire social network, for what?"[9]

Stephen Glass went on to graduate from law school. Would you hire him as your lawyer?

Journalistic Integrity vs. Blind Ambition

For a long time, the *Washington Post*, based in Washington, D.C., has been one of the country's most respected newspapers. Reporters who work there are considered some of the best in the newspaper business. In 1980, the *Post* hired a twenty-five-year-old reporter from Toledo, Ohio, named Janet Cooke to write local stories about life in Washington, D.C. *Post* editors had been impressed with her Ohio experience, her college degree from Vassar, and her reporting awards.

People immediately noticed that Cooke was ambitious and had set high goals for her career. She said she wanted to win a Pulitzer prize within three years. The Pulitzers are considered the top prize in journalism and usually awarded to very experienced reporters.

Janet Cooke wrote a very good story about drug dealers in Washington, D.C. While reporting that story, she claimed she heard on the street about an eight-year-old heroin addict who lived somewhere in the neighborhood. Heroin is one of the most deadly drugs. It is a tragedy for anyone—but especially an eight-year-old—to be addicted to heroin. Cooke told her editors about this boy. They encouraged her to write about him. This looked like a story important enough to appear on the front page of the paper—and every reporter wants a front-page story.

After weeks of research, often on the drug-infested streets of Washington, D.C., Janet Cooke informed her editor that she had found an African-American family that included an eight-year-old addict, his mother, and his stepfather. She called the boy "Jimmy" to protect his identity. She claimed that she saw Jimmy's stepfather inject heroin into the boy while she watched.

On Sunday, September 28, 1981, the *Post* published Janet Cooke's front-page story, entitled "Jimmy's World." Readers were outraged that such a terrible thing was happening. Because Jimmy was African American, some called the story racist, even though Cooke was African American herself. (There are people who believe

Janet Cooke, a reporter for the *Washington Post*, wrote a fabricated story about a very young drug addict. Cooke won a Pulitzer prize, which was later rescinded.

the media too often portrays African Americans as drug users, which feeds into a stereotype of African Americans as drug abusers.)

Readers were also angry at the *Washington Post* for not revealing the boy's real name so authorities could find him and help him. The *Post* would not reveal Jimmy's real name or his address, citing its First Amendment right—the right of freedom of the press—to protect its sources. As part of this freedom, reporters are entitled to protect the identity of their sources; people who might not otherwise come forward. Without cooperation from the newspaper, Washington's mayor and police chief began an intense search for Jimmy. But they could not locate him. The public's outrage continued.

About this time, some of Cooke's fellow reporters and editors in the *Washington Post* newsroom began to doubt that "Jimmy" even existed. Janet Cooke insisted he did. Other editors congratulated her for her hard work and her ability to stand up to the story's intense criticism.

Eventually, the *Post* began to track down leads that followed up on Jimmy's story, figuring if there was one young drug addict out there, there might be others. It was then that other reporters assigned to work with Cooke began to question her about where she had found her story. One went with her to find Jimmy's house, but Cooke said she could not remember where he lived. Other editors began to examine her story more closely. They noticed that the people she had quoted had said things in too perfect a way—that people just do not talk the way Cooke had quoted them.

But most *Post* editors were pleased with her efforts, and the following spring they nominated her story for a Pulitzer prize in feature writing. When the Pulitzer committee announced its awards, Janet Cooke had won. Part of submitting a story for a Pulitzer requires sending a reporter's biography to the selection committee. A biography would tell the selection committee all about Janet Cooke's life before she started working for the *Washington Post.*

When the Pulitzer committee notifies the world of its winners, it also sends out those winners' biographies. When Cooke's biography became public, her former editor in Toledo saw it. He noticed that Cooke had claimed to have graduated from Vassar College. He knew she had not. He knew that she had not attended the Sorbonne, a famous university in Paris, as her biography also stated. He also knew she had not won other journalism prizes, as she had claimed.

The editors of the *Washington Post* were informed that Janet Cooke had fabricated her biography. Once the top editors caught her lying, they finally began to seriously doubt the truthfulness of Jimmy's story—especially since she had never revealed to them his real name and could not find his house. After hours of questioning, Cooke finally admitted that she had made up the story of Jimmy.

Cooke was forced to resign. Her Pulitzer prize for feature writing was awarded to another reporter. Afterward, the *Post* editors analyzed what had gone wrong. Was there too much newsroom pressure for reporters to find sensational, controversial stories for their front page? Was the competition so tough at the top of the newspaper business that reporters would lie to get their stories printed? Was there not a proper system in place that would help editors catch a fabricated story?

The *Washington Post* decided all these things probably played a role, but the person ultimately responsible for this deception was Janet Cooke herself.[10]

Executive editor for the *Post,* Benjamin Bradlee, commented that editors must be able to trust their reporters. He added, "There is no system to protect you [the editor] from a pathological liar, and if you constructed it that way you'd never make a deadline."[11] Janet Cooke's career as a journalist was over. In fact, she faded out of public view, only surfacing occasionally over the years to tell her sad story on a talk show or to a reporter. Then she disappeared from public view completely. Yet she will long be remembered as a reporter who lied to get her story, a person who could not be trusted.[12]

How to Avoid Plagiarism

6

Author Doris Kearns Goodwin is a well-known presidential historian. She appears frequently on television discussing the lives of past U.S. presidents and the behavior of current presidents. In the 1960s, she served as an assistant to President Lyndon B. Johnson, who she later wrote about.

Goodwin's 1994 best seller about President Franklin Roosevelt and his wife Eleanor, *No Ordinary Time*, won her a valued Pulitzer prize. An earlier best-selling book about both sides of President John F. Kennedy's family, *The Fitzgeralds and the Kennedys*, was hugely popular and made into a TV miniseries.

In early 2002, an article in the *Weekly Standard* magazine created a scandal for Goodwin by revealing that she had plagiarized parts of *The Fitzgeralds and the Kennedys*. At first, Goodwin tried to defend herself to reporters. She said that she accidentally lifted a few paragraphs from a book about a Kennedy sister written by a less well-known author named Lynne McTaggert. Goodwin claimed this "borrowing" was due to her own disorganized research procedures, including sloppy note taking.[1] However, borrowing without citing sources is plagiarism, even if it is due to disorganized note taking.

Goodwin did not disclose the whole story at first. Perhaps she was embarrassed at getting caught or afraid of how a plagiarism accusation could hurt her reputation. In her public statements, she left out the fact that several years earlier, she had accused another author of a Kennedy book of plagiarizing from her own Kennedy book, *The Fitzgeralds and the Kennedys*.

Sensing that Goodwin was not telling the whole story, journalists continued to investigate, comparing Goodwin's Kennedy book with the earlier Kennedy book by McTaggert. And they did discover more.

Goodwin had borrowed so many passages from McTaggert's book that she had to pay McTaggert money as compensation. Authors sometimes do this to keep a plagiarism case from going to court. In return for money, McTaggert was not to speak publicly about being plagiarized by Goodwin.[2]

Now, fifteen years later, Lynne McTaggert spoke out to the press because she thought Goodwin had not set the record straight. She claimed that Goodwin used literally thousands of her words. At this point, Goodwin was forced to admit that she had borrowed passages from additional authors for *The Fitzgeralds and the Kennedys*.[3] And she asked Simon & Schuster to destroy all existing copies of the book and publish a corrected version that would give credit to McTaggert's work.

Goodwin experienced consequences as a result of her actions. She resigned her prestigious position on the panel that chooses

Doris Kearns Goodwin, a famous historian, plagiarized another author's work for a book on the Kennedy family. Goodwin claimed that her sloppy research methods were responsible, but her credibility as a historian suffered.

Pulitzer Prize winners. Several universities withdrew their requests for Goodwin to lecture on their campuses.[4] And she was forced to withdraw as a commentator on public television's evening newscast, *NewsHour with Jim Lehrer.*[5]

Goodwin continues to write and sell books and to appear on television programs as a presidential scholar. However, her initial cover-up stories damaged her credibility as a historian. And, in the future, the media as well as rival historians may look more closely at each new book by Doris Kearns Goodwin, searching for more plagiarized passages.

Organize, Organize, Organize

It is easy to see what problems plagiarism, and even being accused of plagiarism, can cause for a professional writer/historian. Many of these problems can be traced, even for experienced people, to their inability to use research properly. If you want to avoid plagiarism, one of the best things you can do is to learn how to use research material—those ideas you look up and refer to when you are writing a paper.

The *MLA* (Modern Language Association) *Handbook for Writers of Research Papers* says, "Because research has the power to affect opinions and actions, responsible writers compose their work with great care. They specify when they refer to another author's ideas, facts, and words, whether they want to agree with, object to, or analyze the source."[6]

Conducting research allows you to gather facts and ideas that have come before and to build those ideas, through your own contribution, into something new. This means you are taking the work of others and adding a new twist to it, a new insight that should be completely your own. There is a lot of research out there, and much of it is available for you to use. But you must always be mindful to cite your sources and give credit to the originator of the ideas and words you are using.

The *MLA Handbook* recommends a system that many students may find useful, which is to first physically organize research into three files. Into the first file should go all of your own original ideas. The second file should contain summaries of the ideas of others—the notes that you have accumulated during your research. The third file should contain the direct quotes that you will use throughout your paper.[7]

The MLA system is just one of several you can use. But find a way to organize your research and writing that works for you. You may create several drafts before turning in your paper, and you want to do everything you can to avoid plagiarizing.

The following suggestions may help organize your work. They can be used separately or in any combination. Or you can invent your own.

- Keep a separate notebook just for your research notes and quotes.
- Use different-colored file cards or file folders to catalog your research.
- Clearly mark direct quotes in your text with yellow highlighter or with any other sign that will remind you that these are someone else's words.
- Never cut and paste paragraphs from your Internet research directly into your paper. Rather, put this research onto its own page and identify its source, then decide how to use it in your text.
- Check the wording of quotes with their originals to make sure they are accurate.
- Carefully examine direct quotes to make sure they add something to your paper.
- Write in the margins of your first draft the origins of your borrowed material.
- Read your final draft very carefully, red pen in hand, to make sure you have attributed all the words and ideas that you have borrowed.

Finally, organizing your time is just as important as organizing your research. Doing homework at the last minute can lead students in a hurry to make mistakes.

When Citing Is Not Necessary

First, it is important to understand when you do not need to cite a source as you write your paper. If something is defined as common knowledge, then you do not need to cite where you got the information. Common knowledge information means you have stated a fact that is generally known, or easily found, in most general reference material like a dictionary or encyclopedia.

For example, if you state that President John F. Kennedy was assassinated in 1963, you do not have to cite your source. That is a fact that many people know. It is a fact that people can easily look up in books and articles. However, if you state that eight out of ten historians believe President Kennedy was killed by one person and not by a group of people who had planned his assassination, then you need to cite where you found those figures.

Citing is not necessary if you are writing about your own experiences, something that happened in your own life. You are your own source and this will be obvious to the reader. In addition, you do not need to cite if you are reporting the results of some activity you have conducted yourself such as a survey or a science experiment.

When Citing Is Necessary

It is absolutely necessary to cite your sources when you are using somebody else's words and ideas, no matter where they came from. They could come from a book, an article, the Internet, an e-mail from someone, an interview, a CD or movie, or the newspaper—anywhere you have found someone else's ideas that you want to use. You also need to cite when you are quoting someone's exact words or any words put together that make up an idea. And it is important to cite any kinds of pictures or charts that you may borrow to emphasize a point in your writing.

Learn to Cite Sources

Learning to use information from a source without plagiarizing is a skill that takes some practice. It also takes an awareness on the part of the student of what belongs to him or her and what is being borrowed. As a student, you will use your research skills all the way through high school and, for many, through college and graduate school. So it is important to learn the basics of the various uses of source material.

There are three ways you can legitimately use other people's writing in your own work. You can *summarize, paraphrase,* or *quote directly*. Recognizing their differences can take some time to understand.

To summarize a passage you have read means to put the main ideas of that passage into a condensed (shortened) form in your own words. A summary is much shorter than the original material. When summarizing, you must cite the original source.

To paraphrase an article or a book means to restate that material in your own words. A paraphrase is usually more detailed than a summary. A paraphrase must also cite the original

One method of keeping your notes organized is by using different-colored folders for different types of research.

source. You must be careful to make clear which ideas are those of the author and which ideas are yours. Paraphrasing does not mean copying almost word for word and using a thesaurus to change some of the words.

If you want to use the exact words from your source material to enhance your own work, then use direct quotes. They must be contained inside quotation marks and then cited. In deciding to use a direct quote, make sure what the quote says will add something of value to your paper.

Stringing Quotes Together Is Not Writing

Some students feel they are actually meeting the requirement of the assignment if their paper consists of nothing but back-to-back quotes. Inserting one quotation after another, even with proper citation, brings no new ideas to the subject. A paper filled mostly with quotes is boring and unoriginal. If the idea in researching and writing is to take the work of others and build upon it, creating something new, then a string of quotes fails that assignment miserably. Practice your paraphrasing techniques so you can put the words of others into your own and in the process avoid using too many quotes.

Practice Using Sources

As an exercise in proper attribution, try summarizing in one paragraph the Blair Hornstine story that appeared in Chapter 1 of this book. Then try paraphrasing in your own words just why exactly she was denied admission to Harvard. Next, write a paragraph about your own thoughts regarding her story and include a quote from Chapter 1. Be sure to cite the source.

A Look at the Legal Side

Northwestern University provides tips for students on how to avoid plagiarism by knowing how to give proper attribution. According to its Web site:

Direct quotes from other writers can add to the quality of a student's work. But crediting the original source properly is very important.

> *In all academic work, and especially when writing papers, we are building upon the insights and words of others. A conscientious writer always distinguishes clearly between what has been learned from others and what he or she is personally contributing to the reader's understanding.*[8]

You have just learned about the various ways to cite a source by summarizing, paraphrasing, or direct quoting. You have learned that using common knowledge or your own experiences does not require citations.

It is also important to become familiar with how the law allows or does not allow the use of creative work that belongs to others. The legal terms you should be familiar with include *copyright, fair use,* and *public domain.*

Copyright laws protect creative work such as writing, paintings, designs, recorded music, architecture, and even computer software. The creative work must be something that exists, such as a book, sheet music, or a computer program. A creative idea, such as a movie plot, cannot be copyrighted and protected if it has not been written down or recorded in some way—offering proof that it exists. No one can use copyrighted material without the permission of the owner of the copyright.

Chapter 2 of this book discussed the first copyright laws in the United States. Throughout the years, Congress has revised copyright law to extend the number of years that a work is protected. Congress has also refined the law to include new technologies such as videotape and computer programs. Copyright law is complicated and constantly changing.

In 1976, Congress passed a law to extend copyright protection. Any material published after 1977 is protected by copyright law for the life of the author plus seventy years. For example, if an author died in 1980, his copyrighted books would be protected until the year 2050. The 1976 revision of the law also created the "fair use" law. This law recognizes that some people might want to use parts of a copyright work for the purposes of commentary and critiquing or for parody.[9]

As an example, a magazine writer who wants to review a book can, under fair use law, quote short passages from that book without obtaining permission from the author. The magazine writer is commenting on the book and discussing whether he or she likes it. However, even when permission is not needed to quote material, it is necessary to say where it came from in order to avoid plagiarism.

A parody makes fun of something in a humorous way. For example, the Austin Powers movies are parodies of the James Bond spy movies. Under the fair use law, the Austin Powers filmmakers would not have to ask permission from the James Bond movie producers or the family of Ian Fleming, the novelist who created the Bond character upon which the movies are based.

Copyrights do not last forever. Intellectual property, meaning a work someone has created, ages and at some point, and by law, loses its copyright protection. When that happens, these works fall into the public domain. This means that no one owns them and the public is free to use them at any time. Any work published in the United States before 1923 is in the public domain.[10] But to avoid plagiarizing, any use of public domain material must be attributed.

Here is an example of public domain. Suppose someone wanted to turn Mark Twain's book *The Adventures of Tom Sawyer*, written in 1876, into a play. That playwright would not have to pay anyone to use Twain's story but would need to acknowledge the source of his or her ideas.

Anything published in the United States after 1977 has copyright protection for the life of the author plus seventy years.[11] Be careful to note, however, what was discussed in a previous chapter: Copyright ownership begins the moment a work is created in fixed form. [12]

If you feel you have written something of value, consider registering your work with the U.S. Copyright Office, which is part of the Library of Congress. You will need to fill out a form and send it, along with a payment and a nonreturnable copy of your work, to the U.S. Copyright Office in Washington, D.C.

How Teachers Curb Plagiarism

In April 2001, University of Virginia physics professor Lou Bloomfield had received and graded homework papers from the students in his Introductory Physics 105 and 106 courses. Bloomfield's popular two-part physics course, titled "How Things Work," draws hundreds of students to his class each semester. Many of these students are not planning to make physics their profession but have a curiosity about how the world around them works.

Students find the course fun. As Professor Bloomfield describes the course, he teaches students how airplanes fly, how televisions work, and why pieces of metal should not be put into a microwave oven. His most famous trick is showing them how to yank a tablecloth off a table without disturbing the things on the table. He calls this demonstration his "story of inertia."[1] But this particular spring, a student approached Bloomfield because she was upset about her grade. Says Bloomfield, "She had some friend or acquaintance who had gotten a better grade than she had. She said that person had used a recycled paper. Somebody else got a better grade on fraudulent work."[2]

Bloomfield required that students submit their papers electronically to a Web site he created. This means that over a period of several years, he had acquired thousands of term papers on his site. He only needed to look through his own files of papers to try to detect plagiarism.

"This whole thing was meant to find a couple of recycled papers," he says. "I was dealing with one specific complaint. I looked for a paper recycled in my class."[3]

It is important to note that the University of Virginia prides itself on its honor system, known at some schools as an honor code, because it is one of the oldest in the country. The school established this system in 1842, over 170 years ago. The honor system states that students must not willfully or intentionally lie, cheat, or steal. The university can suspend or expel students for honor system violations. And students can be punished for breaking the rules of the system up to two years after they have been caught cheating.[4]

To determine if the cheating accusation was true, Professor Bloomfield says he created a computer program that he plugged into the Web site where he stores all his student papers. The program would check the content of these papers to see if any contained the same string of six words as another. The idea was to catch duplicate phrases—meaning phrases that were used more than once.

Bloomfield explained that a two-word string of words might bring up too many false readings of plagiarism, and a ten-word string might not find a match. He says he tinkered around and settled on six words in a row.

"Six turns out to be a long enough phrase. It's pretty unique. It's like a snowflake. Even in our own writing we don't repeat ourselves six words in a string very often," he explains.[5]

Bloomfield decided to submit papers from every student who had taken his course over a two-year period. The results of his test launched what has been called the biggest cheating scandal in the history of the university. He found that more than 150 papers showed possible signs of plagiarism. Students had turned in work, under their own names, that had been copied from others.

The computer, he says, "spit out at least seventy-five pairs of papers with pretty outrageous similarities."[6] The initial six-word string he used to kick off his search helped reveal many instances of plagiarism.

A large number of students now faced the possibility of a very harsh punishment—being kicked out of school. However, the school's honor system was set up to be fair to students accused of breaking it. Students must appear before the Honor System Committee if the committee requests they do so. The committee is not made up teachers, but of students who hear all the evidence and then decide if their fellow student is guilty or innocent.

After the committee investigated the cases, dozens of students were brought to trial. It should be noted that many cases were reviewed and then dropped for various reasons. Some students had been victims of fellow students who had stolen their work. Others had used material from papers that they had written earlier for Professor Bloomfield.

Professor Bloomfield says about the students who were caught cheating, "I was pretty disappointed. There's always a fraction of students who can't get with the program." He says they have that old attitude of "the dog ate my homework."[7]

Many teachers are helping their students understand what plagiarism is and how they can avoid it.

After almost a year and a half of investigations, forty-eight students were found to have cheated outright and left the university. They were either expelled or voluntarily withdrew. Three of these students had already graduated, but university officials revoked (canceled) their diplomas, leaving them with no college degree. All of them must have suffered humiliation, shame, and damage to their reputations.

Preventing Plagiarism

Many teachers resent the time it takes to catch plagiarists, whether they plagiarize off the Internet or the old-fashioned way—from their friends. Playing detective to catch cheaters is not what teachers had in mind when they decided years earlier to dedicate their lives to educating young people.

Jeff Karon, instructor at the University of South Florida, spent many years holding workshops for college instructors about plagiarism. He also spent time on college judicial proceedings, trying to decide what to do with student plagiarists. As plagiarism became easier and easier with new technologies, Karon decided that he "did not want to spend time as a cyber-cop." Instead, he wanted to concentrate on helping students learn to learn with integrity.[8]

Karon developed guidelines for instructors to help them deal with plagiarism. He advocates for a positive solution, one that helps students avoid plagiarism and makes both teachers and students feel stronger.[9] This often begins with providing students with a deep understanding of just what plagiarism is.[10]

More and more teachers no longer assume that students understand plagiarism. They are discussing all the different sides of plagiarism with their classes at a younger age. It is not unusual anymore for eleven-year-old students to learn about it.

Alison O'Donnell teaches middle school in Alexandria, Virginia. She says, "We definitely teach about plagiarism. They [the students] have to cite sources when writing papers." She says that middle school students have a very "narrow view" of plagiarism. She adds that the best thing a teacher can do to help is to "teach them what plagiarism is and how severe it is . . . and how to give credit to other people."[11]

Teachers are talking about plagiarism not with threats of punishment, but with the idea of informing their students of what it is and how to avoid it.

Many teachers have discovered that the best way to help their students avoid plagiarism is to teach them how to manage source material and how to properly cite those sources.

O'Donnell says, "We are teaching them to take their notes properly so if they do need to cite, they have the information they need."[12]

O'Donnell acknowledges that middle school kids have to work at understanding the rules for citing sources. "They're still at an age of determining if it's an author's point of view or a fact in their writing. What the students consider fact is actually something that should be cited. Learning to sort this out is a challenge at the younger level." She adds that understanding what exactly "common knowledge" is when citing sources is also challenging for middle school kids as they write papers.[13]

Overall, she feels that what is most important for a middle school student, whose research efforts introduce them to information they never knew before, is to understand that "you just can't lift information word for word and put it in your work."[14]

Honesty Is the Best Policy

Teachers often appeal to their students' sense of integrity. Someone who has integrity is honest. In some high schools, teachers ask students to turn in their papers along with a signed honor pledge. Honor pledges most often state that students have completed their homework assignments by themselves and not received any outside assistance.

Michael Josephson of the Josephson Institute of Ethics has this advice for students who might be tempted to plagiarize. "Nothing is more important than honor and the ability to claim your own integrity. No grade is worth it."[15]

Challenging Assignments Help Prevent Plagiarism

Student use of Internet term papers has become so common that teachers are forced to browse the online homework sites so they can find out what some of their students are up to. Teachers are getting to know these sites to see what they offer students and to catch suspected plagiarists.

Chip is the student from Chapter 4 of this book whose teacher Ellen Laird caught him plagiarizing off the Internet. Laird believes the new trend of Internet cheating may change how teachers plan their course work. Some teachers will choose not to assign a certain book for a book report, for instance, because reports on that book are all over the Internet sites.

"I worry that these new student practices will shape our reading lists right down to the individual poems we select," Laird says.[16]

In *The Plagiarism Handbook,* Robert Harris recommends that teachers take some steps to prevent plagiarism before it even starts. Harris tells teachers, "The clearer and more specific you make a research paper assignment, the less likely a student will be able to find an off-the-shelf [ready-made] paper that matches it."[17]

Harris recommends that teachers assign papers that ask students to answer specific questions. For example, instead of asking for a paper that explains the themes of the book *Animal Farm,* the assignment instead might ask the student to explain how the themes of that book relate to events today.

Harris suggests that teachers require students to use a variety of resources besides the Internet, such as books, journals, and personal interviews. Another requirement would be for students to submit a complete bibliography (list of sources) they used to compose their paper and evaluate how useful they found those particular sources. He also suggests that teachers require students to hand in printouts or photocopies of their source material.[18]

College instructor Gary Jacobsen described to the *Washington Post* how he prevents plagiarism in his classes by making rules on where his students can find their sources. "I tell my college students, for example, that not more than 10% of their bibliographic references can be from Internet sources. I also tell them that they cannot cite any source older than a certain year (say, 1999)." Jacobsen also requires that his students "submit a companion document that lists where they located all books and periodicals referred to in their term papers."[19]

Teachers Take Action

Most students follow the rules by writing original papers and working hard to properly cite their sources. But there is a growing number of students who will always try to take advantage of the system. The actions of these students have forced teachers and schools to create strategies to catch these cheaters.

Several companies, such as Turnitin.com and Glatt Plagiarism Services, have created computer programs that can identify papers that have been plagiarized. Glatt even offers a CD-ROM that gives instructions on how to avoid plagiarism and tips on how students can detect it in their own writing.[20]

Turnitin.com will compare a student's paper against millions of pages of content the company has access to. This content has come from four sources: (1) any paper available on the Internet, (2) papers that have already been published in books and professional journals, (3) information on Web sites, and (4) over 10 million essays and papers that have already been processed through the Turnitin.com system over the years by students, teachers, and other clients.[21]

Dr. John Barrie formed Turnitin.com in 1996 in Oakland, California. As a student at the University of California at Berkeley, he had seen cheating in his honors classes, "and nothing was being done about it," he says.[22]

A study done on college research papers turned in from 2004 to 2008 demonstrates how plagiarism continues to be a problem. It found that more than 25 percent of assignments had some sort of plagiarism and that 10 percent had a lot of material plagiarised.[23]

Here is a way to better understand these statistics. On average, for every one hundred papers submitted to Turnitin.com, more than twenty-five of them have parts that have been plagiarized. Of those twenty-five papers, ten have been copied nearly word for word.

Turnitin has become more sophisticated since its first text-matching programs. Today it looks at the writing style and grammar of papers rather than relying simply on keywords.[24] It serves more

Many teachers use computer programs to help them detect plagiarism in student papers.

than one million instructors at ten thousand educational institutions world wide.[25]

Some teachers believe that just the threat of students having to run their papers through Turnitin.com prevents a certain amount of plagiarism in the classroom. Barrie agrees. He says that when teachers inform students their papers will be scanned by Turnitin. com, "a massive psychological deterrent kicks in."[26] (A deterrent is something that prevents something from happening.)

Barrie explains it this way. With the millions and millions of papers already stored in Turnitin.com's computer database, students thinking about submitting, for example, plagiarized papers downloaded from the Internet "must ask themselves . . . is it in that database and am I willing to take a chance."[27]

Some teachers say this constant policing of student papers destroys the atmosphere of trust between the student and the teacher. John Walker, who used Turnitin to review hundreds of student university papers, disagrees. He believes that programs like Turnitin can actually improve trust between the student and teacher. He sees plagiarism checks as referees that make sure the teacher has confidence that students are doing their own work and students who do not cheat feel as if they are being treated fairly.

Walker hopes that programs such as Turnitin can help teachers discuss plagiarism in a useful way with students.[28]

Original Work Works Best

Professor Bloomfield, who worked to enforce the honor system at the University of Virginia, has some advice for students writing papers. "If you don't understand what you're writing . . . you're not really learning anything and that should be the point."[29]

Bloomfield believes that the very act of writing forces students to think through ideas and learn. He says, "As a physicist, I find that I often learn more from writing papers and proposals than I do from working in the laboratory. I rarely find writing easy, but I always find it rewarding."[30]

In order to see this, though, teachers must make it clear to the students why they are being given a certain assignment and what the goal of the assignment is. He says that if the teacher asks you to write something about the Spanish Inquisition, the teacher wants you to understand the Spanish Inquisition, not necessarily write the best paper that has ever been written on that topic. He says, "Write the best paper you can write."[31]

8

Fighting Plagiarism Together

Students who plagiarize are not being fair to their fellow students. A student who turns in a plagiarized paper may win an honor that he or she does not deserve. A student who actually did the work might miss out because that grade or that honor was given to someone who cheated. And students who receive top grades from plagiarized papers unfairly raise the level of achievement for others.

Plagiarizing shows disrespect not only toward teachers but toward parents as well, who expect their children to be honest. Students who plagiarize do not respect the hard work of the original author, nor do they respect their hardworking classmates who strive to turn in original work.

Statistics presented in Chapter 1 have shown that a vast majority of students surveyed admitted to turning in as their own other people's homework as well as downloaded information from the Internet. Educators are searching for methods to teach students how to do their own work and why it is important to do so.

Michael Josephson believes that "if plagiarism and other forms of cheating are treated lightly, more people will engage in such conduct more often." He emphasizes that by allowing those who plagiarize to go unpunished, we are dishonoring those who have worked hard and honestly and avoided it.[1]

The founder of Turnitin.com, Dr. John Barrie, worries where cheating may lead a young student. "It's naïve [inexperienced] to think if you cheat your way through high school, you all of a sudden become an ethical person. We're cranking out future leaders of our society who have a shaky ethical foundation. They go on to become Enron executives."[2] (Barrie refers to the large Houston-based corporation that went bankrupt. The name Enron has come to be associated with the worst kind of corporate greed. Executives of Enron admitted to lying and stealing, and some of them went to prison.)

Teachers, students, school boards, parents, and various members of the community are looking for ways to help students resist the temptation to plagiarize.

What Students Can Do

Students should do their best to think originally when composing term papers for an assignment. They should also work to understand the rules for citing the sources they have used in their research. They should make sure they understand clearly what the teacher is looking for in giving the assignment. They should feel comfortable asking the teacher to clear up any confusion they might have about what is and is not plagiarism.

Middle schooler Matthew, who offered his opinions in Chapter 3, says this about plagiarizing. "Most people I know can write stuff on their own without having to copy [from other sources]." He adds that, "The point of writing a report is to understand it. . . . If you're copying from a book maybe you don't understand the topic correctly."[3]

Students need to cite sources not only to let readers know where they got their material but also to give credit to the author of that material. It is important to remember that when in doubt, always cite a source. Also, students should realize that they are responsible for anything in a paper or report that they have submitted with their name on it.

Several Web sites offer students help for writing papers without plagiarizing. Kids Health, for example, gives several tips for making online research easier and ethical. It notes that just "like teachers can recognize your voice in class, most can recognize your voice in your writing." The Web site cautions students that even "accidental plagiarism can have serious consequences."[4]

In addition, the plagiarism checker for teachers, Turnitin, offers a service to students called WriteCheck. WriteCheck will review a student's paper for plagiarism. Students submit their work to WriteCheck and it returns a report that identifies places where the paper may show signs of plagiarism. While many teachers believe this service simply helps students learn to be better cheaters, the makers disagree. They say their purpose is to help students learn to be better writers and avoid plagiarism.[5]

Robert Harris, author of several books about plagiarism, thinks it is important for students to understand the consequences of plagiarism. He says that if the school has a policy regarding plagiarism, the teacher should make sure students know about it. They should also tell students about their own policies. For example, "Cheating

When students understand an assignment and the importance of presenting original thoughts, they are less likely to plagiarize.

on a paper will result in an F on that paper with no possibility of a makeup. A second act of cheating will result in an F in the course regardless of the student's grade otherwise."[6]

One of the best steps students can take is to become familiar with their school's honor code. If their school does not have one, students could suggest to a teacher or the principal that the school create one. Helping to write an honor code may give kids a better appreciation of its meaning. It would also help them understand what is expected of them.

What Schools Can Do

Many schools across the country are working to devise methods of fighting plagiarism, but in a way that emphasizes prevention over punishment. Schools that have created an honor code have made their students aware of their responsibility to academic honesty.

Here is an example of an honor code from a school in Alexandria, Virginia, whose students include those in elementary, middle, and high school: "I pledge that I will not lie, cheat or steal and will not tolerate those who do." It defines plagiarism as a form of stealing.

The honor code also states that "all students must assume responsibility for their own actions, even those beyond the stated requirements of the Code. Therefore, it is expected that a sense of personal honor will direct a student's conduct in all aspects of school life."[7]

Many schools have created guidelines for teachers to follow if they suspect someone is cheating and for students who suspect that another student is cheating.

What Teachers Can Do

Teachers have developed a variety of strategies to help prevent plagiarism in their classrooms. Some of these strategies are "big picture" while others can be very practical. Teachers can:

- Teach students what plagiarism is and why it is wrong
- Encourage original thinking and the forms of good writing

- Teach students to be confident in their work
- Appeal to a student's sense of integrity
- Warn students about the dangers of downloading papers from the Internet
- Create lessons that discuss the proper way to conduct research and cite a source
- Instruct students on how to summarize, paraphrase, and quote sources
- Require students to choose the subject of their papers from a list of specific topics
- Ask students to turn in source notes and outlines so the teacher can see how the students are developing their ideas
- Break the assignment into sections, such as assigning a due date for a first draft

Middle school teacher Alison O'Donnell describes how teachers help students at her school. "We do a lot of our research for projects during class. This is so students can ask questions regarding something they're citing. We check over their notes to see if they have done them properly."[8]

She says she uses a system for note taking that helps the students keep information organized as they go about their research. The students must put the name of each source at the top of its own piece of paper. In the margin of that paper, they write the page number. They start a new piece of paper for each new source they use and eventually turn in all notes for their teacher to check.

O'Donnell's students also edit each other's work. They are instructed to do more than just say the work is good or bad. The student editors are asked to look, for example, for three specific things in a paper to comment on.

O'Donnell also teaches how to use quotations and connect them with the student's work. "If they take a quotation, they have to follow it up with their own idea and explain why that quotation is important. This is a basic way to starting thinking how to use that quotation to support whatever point they're trying to make."[9]

What Parents Can Do

Most parents have a sense of ethics and honor and believe that passing on these values to their children is one of their top responsibilities. Parents also want to have a trusting relationship with their children. Would fewer students download and turn in papers from the Internet if they knew for sure their parents would find out about it?

Ali is a student you met in Chapter 3. Her mother says that students do not learn anything when they plagiarize. She says the best way parents can help students curb plagiarism is to "educate them as to why it's not what they want to do. Sit them down and discuss it with them. To me, it's a moral issue. It's just not right. It's not right by society. It's just not acceptable to be stealing someone else's words. Honesty is the issue here."[10]

One thing parents can do to help their children resist the temptation to plagiarize is to keep current on their kids' schoolwork. If parents know their children have a paper due, they might discuss what plans the students have for their research and outline. Parents can also keep themselves informed of what kinds of citations the teacher expects.

There is another side to the mom-and-dad issue of plagiarism. Parents can actually create plagiarism problems when they become overeager for their kids to do well in school. "Middle school students get so much assistance from home. Parents helping their students is one of our biggest problems in plagiarism," says Rochelle Friedman, principal of a middle school in Northern Virginia.[11] Some parents, so concerned that their children earn top grades, actually want to do the work for them. But turning in a term paper that is partially written by mom or dad is a form of plagiarism.

It is OK to turn to parents for advice and suggestions. That is why they are there. But they might not be as knowledgeable, or up to date, as their children about all the various rules on citing sources and the rules on plagiarism.

Parents who keep current with their children's schoolwork and do not push them too hard to achieve can help fight plagiarism.

Ali's high school brother, Patrick, has some advice for students whose parents want to do too much of their work. "Tell them not to do it because it would be their words and not yours. Be nice to them about it but kind of firm. Say [to them] I need to do my own words to get my own grade. And whatever grade I get you should be happy with."[12]

What the Community Can Do

Here is an example of community involvement in academic honesty. The Josephson Institute of Ethics has long favored "character education" for young people. Character education tries to teach students about what values they share—no matter where the students are from or what else they believe.

Michael Josephson began a movement in American schools in 1993 called "Character Counts!" Josephson gathered a panel of ethics experts together who would identify certain positive character traits. They came up with the "Six Pillars of Character" that make up what Josephson calls core ethical values—values that people might want to use to guide their lives. These values are trustworthiness, respect, responsibility, fairness, caring, and citizenship.[13]

The Character Counts! Movement, observed nationwide in October, is now a coalition, or group, of hundreds of organizations that works to encourage people to think about and make ethical choices in their daily lives.

Character and Plagiarism

Any look at character must recognize that every person is different. Every person has his or her own way of seeing the world and processing information. Every individual possesses unique ideas and a unique voice to be heard. Avoiding plagiarism means working to develop those ideas in your own words, rather than using someone else's. Think about it this way: No one else's plagiarized words can possibly be as interesting as something you thought up yourself.

Chapter Notes

Chapter 1. What Plagiarism Is All About

1. Barbara Kantrowitz and Julie Scelfo, "Harvard to Hornstine: No Way," *Newsweek*, July 21, 2003, p. 50.

2. Editor's Note and Blair Hornstine, "Stories, essays lacked attribution," *Cherry Hill Courier-Post*, June 3, 2003, <http://www.courierpostonline.com/static/st060303g.html> (June 9, 2003).

3. Personal interview with Derek Osenenko, December 9, 2003.

4. Editorial, "Blair, Blair, Blair," *Philadelphia Daily News*, June 6, 2003, <http://www.philly.com/mld/philly/602661198.httm?template=contentModules/printstory.jsp> (October 8, 2003).

5. "Academic Performance," *Harvard Faculty of Arts and Sciences Handbook*, Chapter Two, n.d., <http://www.registrar.fas.harvard.edu/handbooks/student/chapter2/academic_performance.html> (October 8, 2003).

6. Elizabeth W. Green and J. Hale Russell, "Harvard Takes Back Hornstine Admissions Offer," *The Harvard Crimson*, July 11, 2003, <http://www.thecrimson.com/printerfriendly.aspx?ref=348498> (September 19, 2003).

7. Thomas Mallon, Stolen Words: The Classic Book on Plagiarism (San Diego: A Harvest Book, 1989), p. xiii.

8. Associated Press, "A Look at Blair Hornstine's Writings and Other Similar Ones," *phillyburbs.com*, June 6, 2003, <http://www.phillyburbs.com/pb-dyn/news/104-06042003-101885.html> (October 8, 2003).

9. "White House Proclamation, Thanksgiving Day, 2000," *U.S. National Archives and Records Administration*, November 17, 2000, <http://clinton4.nara.gov/textonly/WH/new/html/Mon_Nov_20_-103725_2000.html> (February 9, 2004).

10. Bill Broadway, "Pastor Who Plagiarized Takes Leave," *The Washington Post*, August 18, 2003, p. B1.

11. "Copyright in General," *U.S. Copyright Office*, n.d., <http://www.copyright.gov/help/faq/faq-general.html> (October 7, 2004).

12. "CAI Research," *The Center for Academic Integrity*, n.d., <http://www.academicintegrity.org/CAI_research.asp> (October 13, 2003).

13. Stacy Teicher Khadaroo, "Cheating At Harvard: Probe Focuses on Plagiarism in Era Of Blurry Ethics," *Christian Sceince Monitor*, August 31, 2012.

14. "CAI Research," *The Center for Academic Integrity*, n.d., <http://www.academicintegrity.org/CAI_research.asp> (October 13, 2003).

15. Ibid.

16. "The Ethics of American Youth: 2002 Report Card," *Josephson Institute of Ethics*, n.d., <http://www.josephsoninstitute.org/Survey2002/survey2002-pressrelease.htm> (July 9, 2003).

17. "The Ethics of American Youth: 2010 Report Card," *Josephson Institute of Ethics*, <charactercounts.org/ … /report-card/2010/ReportCard2010_data-tables>, p.130 (November 1, 2012).

18. Ibid., p. 127.

19. Ibid., p. 133

20. Ibid., p. 1.

21. Ibid., p. 7.

22. Ibid., p. 34.

Chapter 2. Borrowing Through the Ages

1. "Plutarch: Priest of the Delphic Oracle," *e-classics*, n.d., <http://www.e-classics.com/plutarch.htm> (April 21, 2005).

2. Thomas Mallon, *Stolen Words: The Classic Book on Plagiarism* (San Diego: A Harvest Book, 1989), p. 4.

3. Ibid., p. 5.

4. Ibid, pp. 4–5.

5. "Intellectual Property: A History of Copyright," Government of the United Kingdom, n.d., <http://www.intellectual-property.gov.uk/std/resources/copyright/history.htm> (October 21, 2004).

6. "Timeline: A History of Copyright in the United States," Association of Research Libraries, n.d., <http://www.arl.org/info/frn/copy/timeline.html> (October 28, 2003).

7. Richard Holmes, *Coleridge, Darker Reflections, 1804–1834* (New York: Pantheon Books, 1998), pp. 208–209.

8. Ibid, p. 280.

9. Kenneth Silverman, *Edgar A. Poe, Mournful and Never-ending Remembrance* (New York: HarperCollins Publishers, 1991), p. 252.

10. Ibid., p. 251.

11. "The 'Basic' Plots in Literature," *Internet Public Library,* November 3, 2002, <http://www.ipl.org/div/farq/plotFARQ.html> (November 16, 2004).

12. Larry J. Sabato, *Feeding Frenzy: How Attack Journalism Has Transformed American Politics* (New York: Free Press, 1991), p. 14.

13. Mallon, p. 127.

14. Personal interview with Laurence I. Barrett, November 10, 2003.

15. Howard Kurtz, "N.Y. Times Article Bears Similarities to Texas Papers," *The Washington Post*, April 29, 2003, p. C1.

16. "Times Reporter Who Resigned Leaves Long Trail of Deception," *The New York Times*, May 11, 2003, p. A1.

17. "Jayson Blair, Certified Life Coach," <http://www.jayson-blair.net/index.html> (November 1, 2012).

18. Julie Bosman, "Jonah Lehrer Resigns from New Yorker After Making up Dylan Quotes for His Book," <http://mediadecoder.blogs.nytimes.com/2012/07/30/jonah-lehrer-resigns-from-new-yorker-after-making-up-dylan-quotes-for-his-book/> (November 1, 2012).

19. Ibid.

Chapter 3. **The Temptation to Plagiarize**

1. Personal interview with Ali (last name withheld), from Troy, Michigan, December 28, 2003.

2. Personal interview with Patrick (last name withheld), from Troy, Michigan, March 4, 2004.

3. Personal interview with Lilli (last name withheld), from Los Angeles, California, March 4, 2004.

4. Personal interview with Matthew (last name withheld), from Fredericksburg, Virginia, March 6, 2004.

5. Robert Harris, *The Plagiarism Handbook* (Los Angeles: Pyrczak Publishing, 2001), p. 4.

6. Ali.

7. Lilli.

8. Ali.

9. Matthew.

10. Patrick.

11. Matthew.

12. "The Ethics of American Youth: 2010 Report Card," *Josephson Institute of Ethics,* <charactercounts.org/ ... /reportcard /2010/ReportCard2010_data-tables> p. 61, (November 1, 2012).

13. Lilli.

14. Ali.

15. Patrick.

16. Ibid.

17. Matthew.

18. Patrick.

19. University of Utah, "ESL Writing Initiative: Plagiarism," <http://www.hum.utah.edu/uwp/ESL/plagiarism.html> (November 1, 2012).

20. Ali.

21. Lilli.

22. Mary Hricko, "Internet Plagiarism: Strategies to Deter Academic Misconduct," n.d., <http://www.mtsu.edu/~itconf/ proceed98/mhricko.html> (June 5, 2003).

23. "The Ethics of American Youth: 2004 Report Card."

Chapter 4. Plagiarism and the Internet

1. Robert S. Boynton, "Is Honor Up for Grabs?" *The Washington Post*, May 27, 2001, <http://www.washingtonpost.com/ac2/wpdyn/A803122001May26?language=printer> (September 19, 2003).

2. Michael B. Farrell, "Why Steal Music When You Can Stream It?" *Christian Science Monitor*, August 21, 2009, <http://www.csmonitor.com/Innovation/2009/0821/why-steal-music-when-you-can-stream-it> (November 1, 2012).

3. Jayson Blair, "Jayson Blair Reflects on Jonah Lehrer's Journalistic Sisn—And His Own," *The Daily Beast*, July 31, 2012, <http://www.thedailybeast.com/articles/2012/07/31/jayson-blair-reflects-on-jonah-lehrer-s-journalistic-sins-and-his-own.html> (November 12, 2012).

4. "Medieval Castles," Bignerds.com, n.d., <http://www.bignerds.com/print.php?eid=773> (January 12, 2004).

5. Ellen Laird, "Internet Plagiarism: We All Pay the Price," *Chronicle of Higher Education*, July 13, 2001, <http://chronicle.com/prm/weekly/v47/i44/44b00501.htm> (October 1, 2003).

6. Ibid.

7. "Superior Papers," <http://www.superiorpapers.com/research_paper.php> (November 12, 2012).

8. "Essay On Time," <http://www.essayontime.com/services/essay.html> (November 12, 2012).

9. Ibid.

10. EssaySite, <http://search.essaysite.com>, (November 12, 2012).

11. EssaySite, <http://www.essaysite.com/buying_essays.html> (November 12, 2012).

12. SchoolSucks, <http://www.schoolsucks.com/>, (November 12, 2012).

13. Personal interview with Michael Josephson, December 10, 2003.

14. David McGrath, "Apathy in Online Education," *Chicago*

Tribune, October 1, 2002, <http://www.chicagotribune.com/technology/chi-0210010171oct01,0,4891014,print.story?col...> (September 3, 2003).

Chapter 5. Plagiarism's Cousin: Fabrication

1. *The View*, WJLA-TV, Washington, D.C., June 17, 2003.

2. "Origin of the word 'Hoax,'" *Museum of Hoaxes*, n.d., <http://www.museumofhoaxes.com/origin.html> (November 30, 2004).

3. "Post Office Calls for Portable 'Vanity' Zip Codes," *All Things Considered*, National Public Radio, April 1, 2004, <http://www.npr.org/templates/story/story.php?storyId=18056551> (November 29, 2004).

4. "War of the Worlds," *Museum of Hoaxes*, n.d., <http://museumofhoaxes.com/war_worlds.html> (November 4, 2004).

5. "Ban Dihydrogen Monoxide!" *Snopes.com*, 1997, <http://www.snopes.com/toxins/dhmo.htm> (July 16, 2004).

6. Adam L. Penenberg, "New Republic Story on Hackers," *Forbes.com*, May 5, 1998, <http://www.forbes.com/1998/05/11/otw.html> (November 9, 2004).

7. Howard Kurtz, "At New Republic, The Agony of Deceit," *The Washington Post*, June 12, 1998, <http://nl.newsbank.com/nl-search/we/Archives?_Action=doc&p_docid=0EB2CCCcc31C2D5B7D17&p_docnum...> (November 5, 2003).

8. Howard Kurtz, "George's Sorry Statement of Affairs," *The Washington Post*, June 8, 1998, <http://nl.newsbank.com/nlsearch/we/Archives?p_action=list&p_topdoc=91> (November 5, 2003).

9. Charles Lane, e-mail to the author, December 17, 2004.

10. Bill Green, "The Players: It Wasn't a Game," *The Washington Post*, April 19, 1981, <http://www.nl.newsbank.com/nl-search/we/Archives?p_action=doc&p_docid=0EB32E182DE96EA3&p_docnum> (November 11, 2003).

11. Ibid.

12. Richard Prince, "Janet Cooke's Hoax Still Resonates After

30 Years," The Root, October 1, 2010, <http://www.theroot.com/blogs/pulitzer-prize/janet-cookes-hoax-still-resonates-after-30-years> (November 12, 2012).

Chapter 6. **How to Avoid Plagiarism**

1. "How the Goodwin Story Developed," *History News Network,* n.d., <http://hnn.us/articles/590.html> (June 24, 2003).

2. Ibid.

3. Ibid.

4. Ibid.

5. Mark Lewis, "Doris Kearns Goodwin and the Credibility Gap," *Forbes.com,* February 27, 2002, <http://forbes.com/2002/02/27/0227goodwin_print.html> (December 9, 2003).

6. Joseph Gibaldi, *MLA Handbook for Writers of Research Papers* (New York: Modern Language Association of America, 2009), p. 52.

7. Ibid., p. 61.

8. "How To Avoid Plagiarism," Office of the Provost, Northwestern University, <http://www.northwestern.edu/provost/students/integrity/plagiarism.html>, (November 12, 2012).

9. "Copyright & Fair Use," *Stanford University Libraries,* 2003, <http://fairuse.stanford.edu/Copyright_and_Fair_Use_Overview/chapter0/0-a.html> (October 28, 2003).

10. Ibid.

11. Ibid.

12. "What is Copyright?" *U.S. Copyright Office,* n.d., <http://www.copyright.gov/circs/circ1.html> (October 22, 2003).

Chapter 7. **How Teachers Curb Plagiarism**

1. Lisa Provence, "Hot Seat—Working Prof: Bloomfield learned how things work," *The Hook,* May 7, 2003, <http://www.readthehook.com/stories/2003/05/07/hotSeatWorkingProfBloomfie.html> (March 2, 2004).

2. Personal interview with Professor Lou Bloomfield, December 4, 2003.

3. Ibid.

4. "Honor Committee Bylaws—After March 1, 2012," University of Virginia: The Honor Committee, <http://www.virginia.edu/honor/honor-committee-by-laws-after-march-1-2012/#IIV> (November 12, 2012).

5. Bloomfield.

6. Ibid.

7. Ibid.

8. Jeff Karon, "A Positive Solution for Plagiarism," *Chronicle of Higher Eductaion*, September 21, 2012, Vol. 59, Issue 4.

9. Ibid.

10. Ibid.

11. Personal interview with Alison O'Donnell, March 8, 2004.

12. Ibid.

13. Ibid.

14. Personal interview with Alison O'Donnell, December 1, 2004.

15. Personal interview with Michael Josephson, December 10, 2003.

16. Ellen Laird, "Internet Plagiarism: We All Pay the Price," *Chronicle of Higher Education*, July 13, 2001, <http://chronicle.com/prm/weekly/v47/i44/44b00501.htm> (October 1, 2003).

17. Robert Harris, *The Plagiarism Handbook* (Los Angeles: Pyrczak Publishing, 2001), p. 44.

18. Ibid., pp. 53–55.

19. Gary Jacobsen, "Curbing Plagiarism," *The Washington Post*, December 6, 2003, p. 25.

20. Glatt Plagiarism Services, http://www.plagiarism.com/, retrieved November 10, 2012.

21. Turnitin, <http://turnitin.com/en_us/products/originalitycheck/content> (November 10, 2012).

22. Personal interview with Dr. John Barrie, January 23, 2004.

23. John Walker, "Measuring Plagiarism: Researching What Students Do, Not What They Say They Do," *Studies in Higher Education*,

February 2010, Vol. 35, No.1, pp. 41-59.

24. Barbara Brynko, "Cross-Cecking Originality," *Information Today*, September 2012, Vol. 29, Issue 8.

25. Ibid.

26 . Personal interview with Dr. John Barrie, January 23, 2004.

27. Ibid.

28. Walker, p.17.

29. Bloomfield.

30. The Plagiarism Resource Site, <http://plagiarism.bloom-fieldmedia.com/z-wordpress/latest-posts/> (November 11, 2012).

31. Bloomfield.

Chapter 8.   **Fighting Plagiarism Together**

1. Illinois Central College, "Library," <http://libguides.icc.edu/content.php?pid=84854&sid=631401>, (November 11, 2012).

2. Personal interview with Dr. John Barrie, January 23, 2004.

3. Personal interview with Matthew from Fredericksburg, Va., March 6, 2004.

4. Kids Health.com, "Take 5: Tips for Life," <http://kidshealth.org/teen/homework/tips/online_research.html>, retrieved November 11, 2102.

5. Elizabeth Murphy, "Plagiarism Software WriteCheck Troubles Some Educators," *USA Today*, September 9, 2011, <http://usatoday30.usatoday.com/news/education/story/2011-09-09/college-cheating-plagiarism/50338736/1> (November 11, 2012).

6. Virtual Salt, "Anti-Plagiarism Strategies for Research Papers, <http://www.virtualsalt.com/antiplag.htm>, (November 11, 2012).

7. St. Stephen's and St. Agnes School, "Honor Code," <http://www.sssas.org/honor>, (November 11, 2012).

8. Personal interview with Alison O'Donnell, March 8, 2004.

9. Ibid.

10. Personal interview with Joanne Jump, March 14, 2004.

11. Personal interview with Rochelle Friedman, February 10, 2004.

12. Personal interview with Patrick, December 6, 2004.

13. Josephson Institute, "The Six Pillars of Character," <http://charactercounts.org/sixpillars.html> (November 11, 2012).

Glossary

attribution—Giving credit to someone or something.

bibliography—A list and description of the works of other authors.

cite—To give a source or quote from something.

copyright—The legal right of control given to someone who creates a work.

credible—Believable.

ethics—The principles of good conduct.

fabricate—To make up something.

fair use—The ability to use and cite small portions of a copyrighted work.

fraudulent—Something that cheats or tricks people.

intellectual property—The products of human creativity, such as books, movies, songs, and designs.

paraphrase—To say or write something in a different way from the original but with the same meaning.

peer pressure—Feeling you have to do something because your friends do it.

plagiarize—To pass off another person's ideas or completed work as your own.

plunder—To seize or rob someone else's things by force.

principle—A standard or rule of good behavior.

public domain—For a creative work, the state of no longer holding a copyright and being available for anyone to use.

quotation—Someone else's word(s) used in another place and enclosed in punctuation marks.

reference—A work such as a book or article that is referred to in order to produce another piece of work.

source—A person or work that provides information.

summary—A short version that gives the main points and ideas of something that has been written or said.

verbatim—Using the exact same words.

For More Information

Copyright Alliance
1224 M Street, NW Suite 101
Washington, DC 20005
(202) 540-2243
https://copyrightalliance.org
e-mail: info@copyrightalliance.org
www.facebook.com/copyrightalliance
Twitter: @copyright4u

The Library of Congress
101 Independence Ave., SE
Washington, DC 20540
(202) 707-5000
www.loc.gov
www.facebook.com/libraryofcongress
Twitter: @librarycongress

Turnitin
111 Broadway, 3rd Floor
Oakland, CA 94607
(510) 764-7600
E-mail: media@turnitin.com
www.turnitin.com
Twitter: @turnitin

Further Reading

Gilmore, Barry. *Plagiarism: A How-Not-to Guide for Students.* Portsmouth, NH: Heinemann, 2009.

Graham, Leland. *How To Write a Great Research Paper: A Step-by-Step Handbook.* Nashville, TN: Incentive Publications, 2007.

Noble, June and William Noble. *Steal This Plot: A Writer's Guide to Story Structure and Plagiarism.* Sanger, CA: The Write Thought, Inc., 2013.

Sonneborn, Liz. *Frequently Asked Questions About Plagiarism.* New York: Rosen Pubishing Group, 2011.

Stern, Linda. *What Every Student Should Know About Avoiding Plagiarism.* New York: Pearson Education, Inc., 2009.

Woods, Geraldine. *Research Papers For Dummies.* Hoboken, NJ: Wiley Publishing, Inc. 2002.

Internet Addresses

Northwestern University. "How to Avoid Plagiarism"
<**http://www.northwestern.edu/uacc/plagiar.html**>

Purdue University Online Writing Lab. "Avoiding Plagiarism"
<**http://owl.english.purdue.edu/handouts/research/r_
plagiar.html**>

U.S. Copyright Office
<**http://www.copyright.gov**>

Index